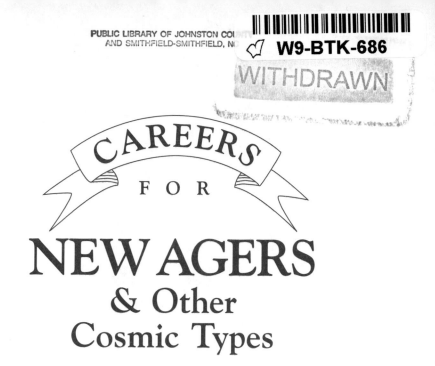

CAREERS

FOR

NEW AGERS

& Other
Cosmic Types

VGM Careers for You Series

CAREERS FOR

NEW AGERS
& Other
Cosmic Types

Blythe Camenson

VGM Career Books

Chicago   New York   San Francisco   Lisbon   London   Madrid   Mexico City
Milan   New Delhi   San Juan   Seoul   Singapore   Sydney   Toronto

Library of Congress Cataloging-in-Publication Data

Camenson, Blythe.
Careers for new agers & other cosmic types / Blythe Camenson.
p.   cm.
ISBN 0-658-00189-2 (hardcover) — ISBN 0-658-00190-6 (paperback)
1. Vocational guidance—Unted States.   2. New Age persons—
Vocational guidance—United States.   I. Title: Careers for new agers and
other cosmic types.   II. Title.   III. Series.

HF5382.5.U5 C25187   2001
331.7'02—dc21   00-66815
                                                                          CIP

VGM Career Books

A Division of The **McGraw·Hill** Companies

1 2 3 4 5 6 7 8 9 0   LBM/LBM   0 9 8 7 6 5 4 3 2 1

ISBN 0-658-00189-2 (hardcover)
     0-658-00190-6 (paperback)

This book was set in Goudy Old Style by ImPrint Services
Printed and bound by Lake Book

McGraw-Hill books are available at special quantity discounts to use as
premiums and sales promotions, or for use in corporate training programs.
For more information, please write to the Director of Special Sales, Professional
Publishing, McGraw-Hill, Two Penn Plaza, New York, NY 10121-2298. Or contact
your local bookstore.

This book is printed on acid-free paper.

To Richard Ryal, who has just
the right amount of New Age
mixed with the solid, old-
fashioned, traditional age, a
hearty thank-you for getting
me started on this project.

Contents

Acknowledgments

The author would like to thank the following professionals for providing insight into their careers in the alternative world of the New Age:

Maggie Anderson, Astrologer

Rev. Jennifer Baltz, Minister, Spiritual Teacher, and Counselor

Cheryl-Lani Branson, Therapist/Career Counselor

Theresa Bulmer, Health Food Store Manager

Robert T. Carroll, Professor of Philosophy, Writer

SuZane Cole, Dream Interpreter

Rev. Paula Cooper, Spiritual Counselor

Elizabeth English, Feng Shui Consultant

Joseph Hayes, Freelance Writer

Joyce Kennett, Bookstore Owner

Charles Lewis, Horticultural Therapist

"Mara," Psychic

Richard Mattson, Horticultural Therapy Professor

James Miller, Yoga Therapist

Joe Nickell, Paranormal Investigator

Victoria Pospisil, Eastern Healing Arts Practitioner/
   Licensed Massage Therapist

Lynne White Robbins, Psychic

Nancy Stevenson, Horticultural Therapist

Abigail Trafford, Writer for the *Washington Post*

Mary Tribble, Event Planner

Roy Upton, Herbalist

Rita Valenti, Tarot Reader

CAREERS FOR

NEW AGERS
& Other
Cosmic Types

CHAPTER ONE

Inspirational Careers in an Expanding Field

"*T*his is the dawning of the Age of Aquarius, Age of Aquarius," or so the song lyrics from the musical *Hair* proclaim. Fact is, no one really knows when the so-called New Age—the Age of Aquarius—dawned, or when it will end.

The composers of *Hair* thought it began "when the moon is in the seventh house and Jupiter aligns with Mars." British astrologer Nicholas Campion gives his own opinion in his book *The Great Year: Astrology, Millenarianism, and History in the Western Tradition*: "It is the shift of the constellations that forms the astronomical basis for the twentieth-century 'New Age' belief in the coming Age of Aquarius, expected to begin when the Sun rises in the constellation Aquarius at the vernal equinox."

When's that? This same astrologer conducted extensive of research trying to answer that question. He found fifty-nine different opinions on when the beginning of the New Age is—from the year 1457 all the way up to the year 3550.

So, maybe the real New Age didn't start in the late sixties or early seventies, as so many of us thought. Maybe it hasn't even started yet and we're still in the Age of Pisces. But something started about three decades ago and is persisting now.

Most "New Agers" are hard pressed to provide a definition for the term *New Age*. Some believe the New Age movement began as an offshoot of the hippie days; others think that it could be a by-product of that time but that it developed on its own, independently.

Some feel the New Age will be a period of greater self-knowledge with a focus on the improvement of the world for all who dwell here. (But, as one astrologer dryly said, "On the other hand . . . knowing Aquarians, I would think there will be millions of started and unfinished projects by the time we are ready to roll into the Age of Capricorn."

Some cynics feel that the term New Age is synonymous with radical thinking; others brand New Agers as far-out flakes. For the purpose of this book, we'll consider New Age to be anything slightly alternative to the well-established mainstream. This covers communications—with and without the benefit of electronic means—alternative medicine and health, merchandising, teaching, spirituality, and the paranormal.

What Makes a New Ager?

To answer this, we must first understand that the whole isn't always equal to the sum of its parts. An interest—whether passing or fervent—in New Age subjects doesn't necessarily mean a person is a New Ager and only that. Just because you check your horoscope every morning doesn't mean you'd visit a Chinese herbalist to cure your stomach ulcer. And though you might have arranged the furniture in your home based on Feng Shui principles, you have no intention of calling a psychic to help you invest your recent inheritance.

Having said that, there probably are some people who embrace every aspect of New Age, who reject mainstream ideas and practices entirely for the nontraditional every time.

How far into the realm of New Age you've stepped doesn't really matter, though. If you're reading this book, chances are you like the idea of turning your avocation into a vocation. Even a foothold in one interest area could be translated to a viable career—a light but lucrative livelihood. These careers appeal to spiritual students who want more adventure in their lives. Such livelihoods are often profitable and gratifying, generating and sustaining a positive, uplifting attitude in both practitioners and clients. We all have to earn a living. So why not do it in a field we love?

The Employment Outlook

In a capitalistic society, one where profit and the bottom line reign supreme, New Age is not just a funky approach to life that old folks patiently tolerate in the young. Early hippies might have eschewed the never-ending quest for the almighty dollar, but today's New Agers aren't as impractical. Business folks and entrepreneurs have long known that where there is an interest, there is a dollar sign, too.

Astrology columns and books, psychic hot lines, metaphysical bookstores, health food stores, and a variety of New Age services and service providers, such as Feng Shui and alternative medicine consultants, abound. Any average American town today is likely to have someone offering psychic reading and astrology classes, past-life regression workshops, and healing lectures. Someone's offering something that is wanted—and making money from it. That's nothing to be ashamed of.

It's the tried-and-true principle of supply and demand. There are needs out there and people willing to provide for those needs. If enough people want little doohickeys in the shape of pyramids or need pouches of crystals for whatever metaphysical purpose, there is no reason someone shouldn't be on the other end, manufacturing and selling this merchandise—and for a profit.

Similarly, it's the people seeking psychic readings or answers from the stars who keep psychic readers in business. It's a relationship grounded in history and not restricted only to New Age. It's how society has sustained itself over time.

The conclusion? The employment outlook will continue to be good—way into the next age—the Age of Capricorn.

Heaven-Sent Jobs for New Agers

A glance through the table of contents will give you an overview of some of the possibilities. The options don't end here, though, and a dedicated career investigator will undoubtedly cover additional job alternatives. Here are just a few to get you started.

Psychic Reader

This covers everything from astrologer and tarot card reader to a "for entertainment purposes only" psychic on a phone hot line.

Mind and Body

This is a huge field, covering nontraditional approaches for the most part, such as acupuncture, armomatherapy, reflexology, Rolfing, Reiki, herbology, hypnotherapy, past life regression, and much more.

Communications

Although the methods of communicating covered in this section are along the lines of the traditional—print, Internet, and so forth—the topics covered are not necessarily so. Closely related to the self-help field, metaphysics has spawned many how-to volumes. These are written by writers, edited by editors, and published by publishers. In addition, there are New Age magazines, newsletters, and other sorts of publications, all needing experienced writers and editors who are in the know.

Throughout this book, in addition to career specifics, you'll find firsthand accounts from real people working in the actual professions. What better way to learn about a calling than straight from the medium's mouth (so to speak).

Do You Have the Necessary Qualifications?

New Age careers range from those that require licensing to those that cannot be legally defined. Each field has its own requirements, and these are covered in the chapters ahead.

It is most important that the New Age enthusiast carry that enthusiasm into his or her work. New Age is almost synonymous with upbeat, positive attitudes. Needless to say, an open mind and a caring attitude will add to your qualifications for most New Age endeavors.

Salaries

Salaries can range from the modest to the glamorous. Some publications, for example, don't pay their freelance writers very much. But psychic hot lines, on the other hand, can charge hefty hourly fees; so do acupuncturists and other alternative medicine providers.

New Agers do not need to undervalue their products and services. Just as in any field, business savvy—knowing how to make money—is important here. With many of the professions covered in this book, the New Age entrepreneur is free to set his or her own fee schedule.

The Job Hunt

For those of you not wanting to start out in your own businesses, let your fingers do the walking—through the Yellow Pages and across your keyboard—as you conduct your on-line searches. Search words such as *jobs* and the name of the field that interests you, such as *New Age publishing*, will bring hundreds and thousands of website listings to your screen.

For More Information

At the end of most chapters and in the Appendix, you will find resources for further information: professional associations you can contact, reference books to consult, and training programs in which you can enroll.

CHAPTER TWO

Insight and Second Sight
Careers for Psychic Readers

W ho doesn't want to know what the future holds or what life is like on the other side? Those with the power (or creativity) to see "beyond" have a huge and eager audience waiting for them.

Psychic Reader is a general term that covers a range of activities. Let's first look at some definitions.

Psychic Phenomena

When referred to in relation to the human mind, psychic phenomena usually fall into two categories: extrasensory perception and psychokinesis.

Extrasensory Perception (ESP)

ESP is the ability to obtain information without the benefit of the five senses. It is usually split into two subcategories: telepathy and clairvoyance. (But you probably already divined that.)

Telepathy is the ability to perceive someone else's thoughts. Clairvoyance is the ability to sense an object or event outside the range of the five senses. In general, someone who can do either or both of the two is considered to be psychic.

Zener cards were specially designed to test ESP ability. A deck consists of a series of five cards, each having one of five symbols—star, square, circle, plus sign, or three wavy lines.

Psychokinesis (PK)

PK is the ability of the mind to influence animate or inanimate matter without the use of any known physical or sensory means. In other words, it is the ability to move or alter matter by thought alone. Psychokinesis includes:

- *Telekinesis*—the ability to move objects

- *Levitation*—the ability to overcome gravity and rise or float in the air

- *Materialization*—causing a spirit or the like to take a bodily form

- *Poltergeist activity*—mysterious events such as rappings, overturned furniture, and flying objects

- *Paranormal healing*—the ability to cure disease or affliction by no known scientific means

Spiritualism

Spiritualism is a system of beliefs focused on efforts to communicate with the dead or with spirits. *Channelers* facilitate communications between the earthly and spirit worlds. Some channelers also attempt contact with extraterrestrials or spirits from ancient mythical societies, as well as with the recently deceased. Channelers are also sometimes referred to as mediums.

Automatic writing is a way for spirits to communicate with earth. A channeler, or medium, will hold a pen and pad of paper, then enter a trance. This allows the spirit to express his or her thoughts, using the medium's hand.

Other Psychic Readings

Other psychic readers might involve themselves in the following activities:

- Astrology

- Tarot cards

- Auras

- Dreams

- Palmistry

- Numerology

Astrology

Astrology is a system that claims the positions and aspects of celestial bodies, such as the moon and planets, have a direct influence on human and other earthly affairs.

Most people are familiar with the twelve signs of the zodiac and, in particular, with the sign that corresponds to the date of their own birth. In the late sixties and early seventies, "What's your sign?" was a common, let's-get-acquainted question. Those who asked it usually knew what the responses meant. "Oh, wow, you're a Virgo? I'm a Taurus. A match made under the stars!"

Astrologers plotting horoscopes based on the exact time and place of birth feel they can produce a very personal reading about the character, strengths, weaknesses, and potentials of an individual and can also predict how all sorts of relationships will work out, including lovers, husbands and wives, friends, and business partners.

Although astrology might have been around as far back as Mesopotamian civilization in 3000 B.C., western astrology did not reach its peak until the influence of the ancient Greeks during 330 to 323 B.C. From there it was adopted into Islamic culture, which later influenced western astrology during the Middle Ages.

Even the rise of the Christian church, which tried to prohibit the interest in and practice of astrology, could not prevent astrology from being used and developed by the populace and important academics. The universities at Florence and Paris, among others, all had chairs of astrology in the late Middle Ages.

The view of creation that resulted from the discoveries of the astronomer Copernicus (1473–1543) led to the decline of astrology and its discrediting as a scientific discipline. Even though most scientists today reject astrology as groundless superstition, interest in this form of understanding human nature remains strong.

And to the astrologer wanting to make a living at this craft, that's good news. Some astrology books routinely become bestsellers. Astrology columns abound in newspapers, magazines, and at on-line websites and on-line services such as America Online.

Almost everyone at one time or another has looked up his or her own horoscope, even if just for a laugh. And then there are the serious believers, who consult the stars on a regular basis before planning day-to-day activities or major life changes.

Astrologers often work privately with these people, doing charts and readings, either through on-line websites, on the telephone, or face to face in home offices or rented office space.

If you have studied the nuances of astrology, have become an expert in the field, and can write, then you can land yourself a column or two or come up with a new angle for a book. Add some private readings to the mix and you can create for yourself a fulfilling part- or full-time career. (Read Maggie Anderson's firsthand account later in this chapter.)

There are several subspecialties of astrology:

- *Event or electional astrology* considers possible dates and times for an upcoming event and chooses the most beneficial one according to aspects of the sun, moon, and planets to the natal horoscope of the person involved.

- *Horary astrology* is an ancient method of divination in which the astrologer constructs a horoscope chart for the time a question is asked and finds the answer in the chart. It's good for all kinds of specific questions that are not answerable via a natal horoscope. For example, the natal horoscope can identify the general area for a career, but only horary can answer a question such as "Will I get the job with XYZ company?" It is also used to find lost objects, animals, and people.

- *Mundane astrology* is concerned with interpreting and predicting public events, such as political and economic developments at national and local levels; natural disasters, such as earthquakes; or man-made disasters, such as the Oklahoma bombing.

- *Natal astrology* interprets the horoscope of an individual based on the date, time, and place of birth. It also compares horoscopes of two or more people for compatibility.

Tarot Cards

The actual origin of tarot cards is not certain. Some believe they first appeared in medieval Europe; others have uncovered legends that suggest they migrated with Gypsies from India. Others believe they are left over from the ancient Egyptian Book of Thoth.

Tarot cards are used by some to get a glimpse of the future; some seek advice in working out problems and weighing decisions. Whether the cards work or not is up to the individual. Any tool that helps an individual seek self-awareness can't be easily dismissed.

Tarot readers work similarly to astrologers, providing their readings electronically or in person. Often astrologers or tarot card readers combine talents and offer services in several different areas, including the following.

Auras

Some people feel that each individual has a visible aura outlining his or her body, an aura that by its color and strength expresses health or sickness, life or death, and so on.

Dreams

Professional psychologists and psychiatrists and laypeople alike are fascinated with dreams. Freud was the first to write about dream interpretation. Those in the traditional helping professions work with clients' dreams; some work intuitively without the need of formal training.

Palmistry

Palmists feel that the lines in the palms of our hands reveal information about length of life, love potential, and other aspects of living.

Numerology

Numerology is a system using numbers to understand human characteristics and perhaps to predict future events.

Firsthand Accounts

"Mara," Psychic

"Mara" worked for three years for the now-defunct Psychic Friends Hotline.

"I prefer to use my stage name because I had problems with clients who bordered on being stalkers. Unfortunately, it's the nature of the business that some people become too attached to their psychics.

"All psychic phone lines use a disclaimer that says they are for entertainment purposes only—to avoid lawsuits—but I consider myself a legitimate psychic. I also gave private readings by phone and in person. Now, I do it for free for friends and family.

"At the time, when I worked for that company, you were screened. You had to give cold readings to interviewers and obtain a recommendation from another psychic. I don't think most companies are that vigilant these days. The Psychic Friends Hotline had pretty strict rules and standards. For instance, you were supposed to discourage callers from staying on longer than twenty minutes, whereas today, the psychics are pressured to keep them on as long as possible! (By the way, I never met Dionne Warwick.)"

Getting Started

"I've always been psychic, or at least I've been as far back as I can recall. When I was about ten years old, I woke up and knew my sister had just had her baby. Minutes later, the phone rang and we were given the news that she had indeed just had her baby. It wasn't something I consciously tried to do or enhance. For several years, I simply ignored it. Then I had other similar experiences, and I realized the ability wasn't going to disappear.

"In college I helped raise money for the arts by giving readings to strangers at a street fair. I realized then that my abilities had strengthened and focused. I found myself giving very specific details, such as where someone's father lived, why they were estranged, what the person's hobbies were, and so on.

"I never even asked their names; the information just flowed. But lots of times, I only picked up vague impressions, and there were times when nothing came to me at all. I found it odd, and occasionally disturbing, but mostly I tried only to read people when asked.

"I'm extremely careful about respecting privacy. And, of course, like most people, I can rarely read for myself. I only pick up on certain things, and no, I've never picked the Lotto numbers (sadly).

"Due to an illness, I was forced to work from home, and a friend suggested I start giving private readings. I was bored and lonely, and it sounded like something positive I could do. During my research into the private-reading sector, I met a very talented psychic who directed me toward the Psychic Friends Network."

What the Work Was Like

"As a psychic, my duties involved answering specific questions as well as giving information that I picked up that didn't have to do with questions asked; I also had a long list of resource numbers that I gave out when a caller had certain crises, such as domestic abuse, substance abuse, depression, and so on.

"We made it clear that we were not the end-all, be-all answer to all problems. We were very conscientious about directing people to the nonprofit organizations that could help them. Along with spiritual guidance, we all believed that real-world solutions were very crucial. We had to be very responsible about not instilling blind faith in our abilities. Instead, we tried to help our clients help themselves.

"We psychics were there to help, not to play God. I saw myself as someone who tried to shine a little light and show people the different pathways they could take. I firmly believed (and still do believe) in free will. I told people I was not 100 percent accurate and that, at most, I could claim 75 percent to 80 percent.

"If I couldn't read them (which rarely happened), I'd immediately let them know, so that they could move on and call another psychic. If they were unhappy with their experiences, they were issued a refund.

"I worked from home and kept a separate phone line. I'd log on for at least four hours a day, and sometimes as many as eight. Sometimes, calls would flood in, and other times it would be quiet and boring. Late nights were usually very busy. I kept logs of all of my calls, recording names, birth dates, the nature and length of the calls. Full names and addresses were only used if the callers wanted to get the free psychic newsletter; otherwise I'd simply write down a first name. Confidentiality was very important, and no one but the caller and I knew what the calls were about. Since I had repeat callers, I'd make sure I'd record when they planned on calling next, so that I'd be on duty at that time. Otherwise, they'd be disappointed. Repeat callers were important, but we were instructed not to let them call us more than once a week. It wasn't just the cost of the calls, but the possible dependency issue. Clients could become addicted to the psychic lines. We were supposed to prevent that and notify the company if anyone became a problem. They could be blocked if this happened.

"Working from home sounds idyllic, but in truth, I was a 'slave' to the phone. I absolutely had to pick up by the third ring, and I always had to be 'on,' meaning I had to be open, empathetic, and positive, no matter what domestic crisis I was right in the middle of. If friends called on the other line, they'd know I often had to hang up on them with little more than a good-bye. The same went for visitors and household chores. Family members, especially, had to be compliant or it wouldn't work.

"My hours were flexible but odd. My schedule would vary from week to week, and it was all up to me to choose the times I was logged on."

Upsides and Downsides

"I really enjoyed talking to so many intriguing, complex people; no two people were the same, though most of their questions revolved around three subjects: health, love, and money. So many of the people were sincere and truly seeking guidance. I was touched by the courage so many displayed despite their often heartbreakingly difficult lives. I heard more tales of sorrow and desperation than I'd ever dreamed of. I also heard tales of great love, sacrifice, and selflessness. The job opened my eyes and heart to the wide spectrum of the human experience. The greatest joy I felt was when I reached someone or helped someone in some small way.

"I remember when I told a woman that I felt concerned about her husband's health. (I never predicted diseases, death, or anything so extreme, but I felt a sense of pressure in the chest area.) I urged her to talk him into seeing a medical professional, which I clearly told her I was not.

"She called me back a week later and thanked me. She took her husband in that day, and they were able to stop a heart attack that might have killed him.

"I also enjoyed the moment when I told a young woman that she'd be getting a job offer any moment; just then, she was beeped by Call Waiting. It was the job offer she was waiting for! Naturally, I was thrilled for her.

"Then there were those less concrete moments when a client would tell me that they felt better—lighter after my readings, even though nothing had really changed in their lives. I felt humbly pleased that I could help if only in a small way.

"My repeat customers were also joys. I could never give them private readings or step over the professional boundaries, but I felt a real bond with them. I often wished we could be friends, though I knew it wasn't possible. I think of them often.

"The downside was when no calls would come in and I'd be waiting. Nothing is lonelier than a silent phone. I also agonized over my obsessive callers, those who were locked in torment over unrequited love. Nothing I said ever got through to them. One woman had put her whole life on hold for ten years for a radio personality she'd met once or twice. She hadn't spoken to him or seen him since, but she was convinced he'd someday realize that he loved her and would come and sweep her off her feet.

"I also talked regularly with a wealthy man who was destroying himself over a woman who'd married another; he was consumed by his need to get her back. Nothing I said ever reached him. He was also seeing therapists, whom he ignored as well. None of the obsessives could let go. It was absolutely tragic.

"I also grieved when I spoke to a caller whose life was so deeply unhappy and who'd suffered so unfairly that I wanted to force the Fates to make things better for her. I am still haunted by the saddest cases.

"Once in a while, I'd receive prank calls, but they were rare. I'd promptly report them to the company. I also on occasion received hostile calls. People would actually take the time and money to try to confound the psychic. They were calling to disprove psychic phenomena and were often angry if you actually saw through them.

"Occasionally, I answered calls from individuals who could only be described as dark. One sweet-voiced young woman told me of how in her past she'd committed a heinous crime and how she'd only been sentenced to a few years of prison time for it. She giggled a little as she confessed that she knew she'd really gotten off easy. Luckily, those chilling calls were very rare. Thankfully, I never had someone confess to a crime they hadn't paid for."

Salaries

"This may surprise many, but we psychics made little money. As independent contractors (which meant we had to pay our own income and Social Security taxes), we grossed about twenty dollars per hour. I've heard that the rate is much lower these days. Sounds like a lot, but you realize the psychic had to have been giving readings for that entire hour. You were not paid for simply being logged on, only for actual talk time.

"The most I ever grossed was a thousand dollars one month. I usually averaged about three to four hundred dollars gross per month.

"Some people logged on more and made more, but they also burned out faster because readings take a lot out of you."

Advice from Mara

"Make sure you are doing this because you feel you have the gift and have the genuine desire to give to others. You won't get rich, as a rule, doing this job.

"To start out, attend New Age festivals and talk to professionals. Reading books can help, but I feel you learn the most from other psychics.

"Let a few psychics read for you and listen to what makes you feel 'right' and what doesn't.

"Never give gloom and doom readings or dark readings. Most psychics concentrate on the positive, even if they see something that could be negative. Nothing is engraved in stone, and psychics can always be wrong. You can try to open some doors for people, to show them the possibilities, but you can never play God. I believe all people have some degree of psychic ability, and you can develop your own."

Lynne White Robbins, Psychic

Lynne White Robbins has worked as a professional psychic, most recently through the Crystal Ball Forum on America Online (AOL).

How It Works

"The Crystal Ball Forum is one of the channels of AOL and features 'rooms' for live, on-line psychic readings, including tarot, clairvoyance, clairaudience, astrology, clairsentience, and even dowsing and pendulums.

"One of the divisions of the Crystal Ball Forum places professional psychics under contract, manages reading requests, and offers a choice of a 900-line service, a live on-line service, or E-mail readings. Prices are reasonable, and clients are given completely private readings."

Getting Started

"For this kind of work, experience has been the best teacher. Although I have a master's degree in education and a bachelor's degree in psychology, learning to read psychically has been a very personal journey. It has meant taking courses—in astrology and holistic theories—and studying theories about tarot and various kinds of spreads and throws. It has meant learning the significance of different decks and understanding what deck might be best for which kind of reading or situation.

"In addition, there have been hours and hours of practice, with clients throughout the country, both in person and over the Internet. I have had to gauge the accuracy of readings based on client comment and reaction, and I try to gauge what I might need to work on or focus on to become more accurate or insightful or helpful.

"I've taken most of my courses and workshops through a foundation in my area that offers many different types of workshops in holistic and New Age foundations.

"I think I began this work when I was a child and was able to 'see' people that other people did not. One such person was a Native American woman wearing formal costume (fringed sleeves, a hair band) and sitting with a bowed head reading or looking at something in the living room of our home! Many years later, I read that a Native American tribe had once occupied the land that the house was built on.

"For many years, I did not know what to make of this talent. I did readings whenever the opportunity presented itself because I was as curious about it as the people I read for!

"For several months, I corresponded through E-mail with one of the readers at the Crystal Ball Forum who had done a reading for me. I ended up reading for them, and they were satisfied with the reading.

"To get the job for the Crystal Ball Forum, I had to agree to do off-line readings as a volunteer. Off-line readings were E-mail readings that AOL clients mailed to a central post office at the Crystal Ball, with various questions for the readers. As time went on, I took training through classes offered by Crystal Ball staff in how to be a room host, how to handle offensive or disruptive clients, and so on. I was mentored before I actually went on-line as a room reader. I remember the day that I was to go on I got a huge splinter in my thumb, which made it very difficult for me to shuffle the tarot cards!"

What the Work Is Like

"I began working formally for the Crystal Ball on America Online about 1994 or 1995. I happened upon the room while looking for information on the tarot, visited, and had a reading done. Then I set about finding out how I could become a reader as well.

"I am psychic and was looking for ways to use this ability on-line. During some of my first readings I was stunned at how much information could come over on-line—the fact that I could conduct readings on-line, over the telephone/modem wires, or even just through E-mailed questions, without even meeting the people, knowing what they looked like, or where they were from. Often very strong impressions come through based on words, sentences, or even conversations—the more focused the question, the stronger the impressions.

"One of the first readings I did was for someone whose husband was waiting to hear about receiving clearance from a medical review board thousands of miles away in Hawaii. I saw that he would receive the clearance as well as news of impending employment—and events proved it to be true.

"Another incident was with members of a psychic lost-and-found team for the Crystal Ball's psychic investigations unit. Not only was the team able to zero in on the person's surroundings and her kitchen, including what was cooking in it, but they were able to zero in on that person's situation in years past, in another environment, and in specific detail. No one on the team was given any information that would have informed them of specifics in any way."

Maggie Anderson, Astrologer

Maggie Anderson makes her living as an astrologer, astrology teacher, and astrological writer. She learned her craft through beginning and intermediate astrology classes in the Community Education Department at Kirkwood Community College in Cedar Rapids, Iowa.

She's had additional astrological training at professional conferences, and she belongs to the International Society for Astrological Research (ISAR), the Association for Astrological Networking (AFAN), and the Astrology Association of Great Britain (AAGB). She founded the Ascella Mundane Astrology Club.

In addition, she has an associate's degree in addictions counseling, a bachelor's in sociology, and a master's in marital and family therapy. She's been working in the astrology field for more than thirty years.

"I work from my Mount Vernon home in Iowa. I give astrology readings in person, by telephone, or I place them on a tape that I mail to the client. Occasionally, I will go to a client's home or office if circumstances require it, but then I charge for travel time.

"Writing as AstroMaggi, I write columns for Astronet on America Online (Keyword: Astronet), Women.com, and Yahoo!

I write several columns, including 'BirthdayScopes,' 'Humor-Scope,' 'Stars on Stars' celebrity profiles, and a weekly 'Your Unique Horoscope,' which is available by subscription through Astronet's weekly newsletter. 'HumorScope' is now in print syndication through United Media Syndication. I also write for another site, StarIQ, and a New Age magazine, *Sowell Review*.

"I now give readings each month at a New Age bookstore, Journeys In, in Marion, Iowa. I hold astrology classes in my home and other locations convenient to the students. If a student is willing to organize a group of friends or coworkers interested in studying astrology together, I will go to their homes or offices to teach classes.

"Approximately every three months I hold a special-topic, all-day workshop in my home. I lecture on astrology in a variety of settings, usually within a fifty-mile radius of my home."

Getting Started

"My interest in astrology began as a result of my becoming aware of the correlation between birth dates and occupations. I worked the night shift in a personnel department of a large aircraft factory in the sixties. I had access to hundreds of personnel files and security clearances and had several hours each night with little to do but explore the files. As a budding sociologist, I tallied everything in those files, from number of marriages and divorces to the variety of health problems.

"Finally, I began to tally birth dates and noticed a distinct correlation between occupation and sun sign. For instance, 100 percent of administrative staff in the department I worked in were Virgos, and 78 percent of the electricians were Aquarians, a sign ruled by Uranus and associated with electricity. The mechanic's birth dates were divided almost equally between Aries and Scorpio, which I later learned are both ruled by Mars and connected with mechanics.

"I was quite impressed with those findings and began to study astrology on my own. I took classes later.

"My original plan was to go into career counseling and use astrology as a diagnostic tool. I felt it could provide valuable insight for individuals looking for direction in their work, so I began my studies with this in mind. I began doing charts for friends and neighbors, and then, several years after I first started studying astrology, I received requests for charts from the public through word-of-mouth advertising only.

"I had several false starts, though, at full-time practice. My need for steady income and benefits led me to work in other areas and work in astrology only part-time. My own career path did include career counseling and work in various social service areas. No matter where I've worked for 'real money,' however, I've continued to practice astrology part-time and use it as a diagnostic tool with clients in my other work.

"Now I'm a full-time astrologer who also provides career consultations as a subspecialty. My private practice comes primarily through referrals and advertisements in the Yellow Pages. I have also placed business cards and flyers for classes and workshops in area bookstores, and I send E-mails to interested parties. To generate repeat business, I keep a running record of previous clients' birth dates and send them a reminder when it's time for an updated progressed and solar return chart reading.

"New clients receive a current fee schedule, a list of services, and several order forms for additional services. At the beginning of each year, I mail clients, students, and others who may be interested the next year's calendar, with Mercury retrograde periods highlighted.

"Twice a year I send mailings to students and potential students with a list of upcoming classes and workshops. As time allows, I generate mailings to organizations that might be interested in having me as a guest speaker, and sometimes I follow up with a phone call.

"I began holding classes at the request of some clients, and that work has grown considerably. The job with Astronet came as a result of a referral from a friend, another astrologer who was working in one of their chat rooms. He discovered they were looking for a writer and suggested I submit sample columns. I did and was hired."

What the Work Is Like

"There's a great deal of variety in being self-employed as an astrologer. No two days are ever the same, so I'm never bored. I set aside about a day and a half for writing at the beginning of the week because there are deadlines to meet. Appointments for readings and classes are scheduled around the deadlines. I take evening appointments several nights a week as well as Saturday, and occasionally I give a reading in a client's office or home.

"I offer a series of eight-session beginning, intermediate, and advanced classes twice a year and usually have students taking private lessons as well. Promoting astrology to the general public is important, so I've developed six lectures I give in a variety of settings. I also founded and coordinate an area astrology club, Ascella Astrologers. Last month I spoke at the local nature center on moon madness, the seventh and eighth grade classes at a Catholic school on moon lore, and at Barnes & Noble on children of the zodiac.

"I try to keep reasonably busy without becoming overextended, and I aim for a forty- to forty-five-hour week. There have been weeks when I've put in eighty hours with astrology work and others when I've had family and other obligations where I've only worked ten. Winters in Iowa can be ferocious, so I never schedule classes or workshops from December through mid-March, and I tend to do more phone consultations and planning during these months.

"To do an astrological reading, I first make a horoscope chart, which is the map of the heavens at the time and date the person was born, as seen from the location of their birth. I have a computer program that will produce a chart in several minutes. Hand calculating and drawing the chart takes about twenty minutes, so having a computer is a real help.

"I interpret the chart and make notes on important patterns, majors themes, and future trends. I either make a tape for the client and mail it or do the reading over the telephone at a prearranged time. If I find something new in a chart, I'll go to the books and do some research.

"I'm a traditional astrologer and have a nice collection of older astrological texts. My primary resource is the work of William Lilly, *Christian Astrology*, written in 1647, and the writings of some of his contemporaries.

"If I'm seeing a client who is experiencing difficult problems, I'll make a point of updating my list of potential referral sources. I maintain a relationship with a former employer in the mental health field and consult with her whenever I have a client who is especially problematic, so I can direct that person to the right place to get help.

"I'm a morning person and so am often at work by 7 A.M. in my study. I'm really very fortunate to be able to work at something I enjoy from my home."

Upsides and Downsides

"The thing I appreciate most about being an astrologer is that all of my clients are voluntary clients! This is in stark contrast to work in the human services field, where approximately 80 percent of clients are mandated to counseling by the court, school system, or employers. I'm able to provide a desired service that the person I'm dealing with directly really wants.

"There is a great deal of flexibility in my schedule. If I want to take a day off and work in the garden, I'm able to do it. If I'm needed to care for a sick grandchild, I can be helpful to my family and still manage the work flow.

"The downside of working alone is the isolation. Since some of my work is done on the telephone or taped, there are days when I don't see anyone but my three dogs and two cats!

"Astrologers have a reputation for being very independent, so whether in the city or country, most work alone. The Internet has promoted networking among astrologers. I've met several others in the state through an on-line service. We exchange E-mails, talk on the phone, and get together in person several times a month. I keep in touch with what's going on in the astro-logical community through various professional publications, Internet mailing lists, and newsletters. I do volunteer work and meet friends for lunch and so am not exactly housebound or lacking for human contact."

Salaries

"My income is generated from several sources and is variable. Writing brings in about $600 a month. Classes and workshops bring in anywhere from $4,000 to $5,800 per year. Sales of com-puterized reports generate about $2,000 annually. Most income is from readings. I charge $80 for a natal chart and $50 for an updated progressed and solar return reading. Low for a week would be two readings at $160, and the most I'd do is ten, bring-ing in $800. Some astrologers can and will do many more than that per week. Five to six readings is average for me.

"Beginning astrologers should find out what the going rate for a reading is in their areas. In rural areas fees are very low compared to the city. Between $200 and $300 for a ninety-minute reading is a fairly standard fee for an astrology reading in a large metropolitan area. Of course, someone with a 'big name' in the field can command even more. Several astrologers in the Chicago area charge $500. It's a matter of supply and demand like anything else."

Advice from Maggie Anderson

"Most astrologers begin by interpreting charts for family and friends, then branching out with some free or low-cost services to friends of friends. After enough training and experience, you can develop a part-time practice that could grow to provide enough income to live on.

"I believe astrologers should have training through the advanced astrology level, either through local classes or correspondence courses, plus several more years of study and experience doing many charts before working with the general public. A year or more of college-level counseling classes would also be helpful. Many people approach astrologers for a reading at a critical times in their lives when they are experiencing some very serious problems. If you open your doors to the public, a few who enter will be mentally ill, alcoholic, or drug addicted.

"Some will be overly dependent, 'perpetual clients' with very poor boundaries. It's important to have strategies to deal with these types of people or your practice of astrology will become secondary to managing problematic clients. A primary reason given by hobby astrologers for giving up working professionally in the field after a few months is that they had difficulty dealing with these particular members of the public.

"As in any other independent business, you need to become proficient at self-promotion. You can do this by giving free public lectures, teaching classes, and writing articles about astrology for local publications. Advertising may or may not be necessary, depending on how large a practice you wish to have. If astrology work is going to be your primary source of income, advertising widely is probably a necessity.

"Location is important, too. Larger cities have a greater number of potential clients to draw from, and you can charge higher fees. You need to operate from a location that is accessible to clients or learn to love working over the phone and the Internet."

Rita Valenti, Tarot Reader

Rita Valenti works from her home on a part-time basis, giving readings on-line and over the phone. Currently, she is involved with an on-line forum called Crystal Visions.

She has bachelor's degrees in English and industrial psychology and has completed the necessary classroom hours for certification as a counselor.

Getting Started

"My work was never really 'started'—it always was. Some people define work and an exchange of services for dollars; this work is more like a calling. The idea of this work was, in fact, very unattractive to me at the start. As a child I always played with cards. I named the court cards, built houses, and developed stories about who they were and what adventures they were on.

"When I was about four, the phone rang, and I said, 'Pop died.' Pop was a very old man who was a friend of the family. The call was, indeed, a message about Pop's passing. There were one or two more incidents like this over the next year or two.

"When I was in first grade, the teacher accused me of cheating when we played games because I knew the answers to questions before they were asked.

"We also played a game in which one team member had to secretly select someone from the classroom floor to play in his or her place. It was with this game that I first tried 'willing' something to happen. I would select one of the players and mentally will them to select me. It happened more often than not, and, by the way, that teacher was also sure I somehow cheated.

"This got to be more of a problem than a gift. I not only had to defend myself to my teacher but to my parents as well. I knew better than to speak of voices, willing, or visions, lest I spend some time locked away.

"I set aside the ability to see, but as I grew older (with the flower children of the sixties), I developed an interest in astrology, numerology, and general areas of divination without the mind-altering stimulation that often went along with such discoveries during that period of time.

"In my late teens, I found that when I had a pen in my hand and was not thinking, I would doodle some pictures, but I would also write out 'August 8th' or '8/8.' This date had no meaning to me. Soon afterward, I began waking up on Saturday mornings with tears in my eyes. There was no dream or upset to set my tears in motion.

"Years later, early one morning the telephone rang. As my husband reached to answer it I told him, 'My brother is dead.' It was Saturday morning, August 8. That was the message we received. My brother, a healthy eighteen-year-old, was killed in an auto accident. They were driven off the road by a drunken driver.

"There was no doubt that there was something different about me, but I did not want that to be seeing death. In my prayers and meditations I asked not to be able to see death, unless there was something I could do to change it, such as offer a warning or send someone to see a medical professional.

"For many years, I would pick up the cards just once in a while and read for a friend. I met a reader in Salem who said it was time for me to come back—without knowing I read. I began working in this field again.

"In 1994, I discovered America Online. I never imagined so many people would be looking for readings (free ones, of course). I found the only forum on-line that was doing readings and soon became a member of that group. I stayed for a while but eventually stopped reading there. I, of course, have read off-line, and I continue that practice. I also read on the telephone—but never for any 900 numbers. I also read in front of groups of people who want to provide entertainment to their guests (Halloween seems to be the busiest time).

"Currently I help out with a community of on-line readers called Crystal Visions. I read when a staff member is unable to make a shift, and I share in some of the administrative work. I have now developed a following. Those people for whom I read come back year after year. As with any profession, you have to spend lots of time developing a client base."

What the Work Is Like

"I am a psychic tarot reader. I sit with clients and look into the past, present, and future, offering insights into the options they have for decision making. I also teach the intuitive method of tarot reading and give lectures and workshops to small groups on- and off-line.

"The job can be intense. I feel responsible for the information I relay to people. A good reader never offers advice—only options. The final decision is always up to the seeker.

"I am a channel. I am an empath. I see, hear, feel, smell, and taste the messages my guides receive for the seeker. I use the tarot cards as a map to direct me to where in the seeker's life the message I receive falls.

"Doing a channel-type reading is draining. It takes concentration and focus and at the same time, you cannot cross to a point where your thoughts are dominant.

"My day is structured and at the same time quite flexible. I can schedule appointments that fit in so that I do a certain number of readings per day and per week.

"I usually work at night on-line. I sign on and check that there is someone in the chat room to read or greet those who visit. If not, I fill that spot. The room is usually busy, and maintaining some type of order is often difficult. Most people are considerate of those fortunate enough to make the list for that evening.

"For my work at home, I have to prepare and make sure I will not be interrupted. Usually I try to clear my mind beforehand and try to relax. I focus on my feelings for a while before the appointed time. It will often take me an hour or so after hanging up to clear my mind of thoughts from this reading.

"The hours are sometimes difficult because of time zones. I have had situations where a friend (usually my clients become my friends) calls me in the wee hours of the morning—perhaps because of a family problem or because they are upset about an issue. I never say I am too busy, and this is never treated as a business arrangement."

Upsides and Downsides

"There are many joys to the profession, including sharing happy events and offering encouragement to those who just have to hear from someone else that they could do it!

"I do not give medical or legal advice; I leave that to the professionals. But I have suggested to people that they see their doctors when I feel there is some danger or need for medical attention.

"One person heeded my advice and was scheduled for a bypass almost immediately. I have told people they were pregnant when they did not know. And I have even, more than once, specified date of birth and gender before the parents knew they were expecting.

"I do not like being associated with scam artists—those who claim they can read and only do it for the money, those who play on what I call the three Gs: greed, guilt, and grief, and convince people they need high-priced spell-removing nonsense.

"Some people begin to depend on readings to make decisions in their everyday lives. I try not to deal with 'reading addicts,'and my policy of not reading for the same person more than once every three months usually keeps them away."

Salaries

"Because you are in your own business, the sky is the limit. Most readers when starting out read just to confirm they have the ability. Readers for 900 numbers do not earn what the seeker is charged; some earn a by-the-minute charge—usually twenty to thirty-five cents.

"Some readers charge a flat fee for a service; that can vary depending on what the service costs. Some well-known psychics charge $500 or more per hour, and I have heard of a channel who speaks to those who cross over who charges $2,000 a session.

"I never charge for the reading—only for the time I spend. And even then I can sit for two hours talking but will only ask for compensation for the actual reading time.

"My rates vary between new clients and older clients, and for that reason I usually do not publish them. The going rate for the time spent on a reading seems to fall between $25 and $100 per hour, depending on the location, the method of reading, and the reader.

"When and if someone needs a consult and cannot pay for it, then I will provide them with a reading free of charge.

"New readers have to build up a clientele that feels confident in the reader's abilities. That might require doing some freebies or working with a group of readers. The work I do on AOL is mostly for advertisement. I get paid referrals from there."

Advice from Rita Valenti

"Any reader who reads because he or she felt pushed to do so by some unknown force is actually answering a spiritual calling; it is compelling, and you will do it regardless of other callings in life.

"If you are a people person, you can meet wonderful people on-line. Learn about people. Learn about different belief systems and cultures. Be willing to accept that there is no right and wrong; it is not up to you to judge—only to relay information. You have to realize you are a tool in the greater scheme of things.

"Although you can earn a good living doing this, be prepared to give of yourself. Reading is not just knowing the face meanings of a tarot deck."

SuZane Cole, Dream Interpreter

SuZane Cole works from her home and does her dream work with clients on-line and through E-mail. She has been working professionally since 1999.

Getting Started

"I have been intuitive all my life. As I grew older it became stronger. After my youngest son, age twenty, passed over in 1994, my abilities grew nonstop, and I began to seek ways of putting these abilities to work for the good of all. I began to listen and follow the direction of my spirit guides, trusting them more and more as the days went on. I was attracted to the fact that I could do this; it just came easily to me, and dreams have always fascinated me. People would speak of their dreams, and as I listened, I just *knew* things.

"An on-line friend of mine knew of my abilities and began to refer people to me who wanted help with their dreams. As time progressed, this friend and I chatted more and more. She then asked me if I would do a dream reading session on-line for a company called Crystal Visions. I agreed and followed the flow in that direction."

What the Work Is Like

"I spend approximately three hours a week—an hour and a half, two evenings a week—in a monitored on-line chat room on America Online where I do dream interpretations for people. But the amount of time can vary if I get dreams sent to me via E-mail, asking for an interpretation.

"I have a very talented hostess who sets up a list of the people in the room who want a dream reading done. When it is the next person's turn, he or she has fifteen minutes to tell me about the dream. I then interpret the dream, using information that comes from a combination of universal dream symbols and my spirit guides.

"There are nights when I stay on to chat with people in the room; fifteen minutes is not a very long time. At times, there are some who need more information than I can honestly give them in that time, so I spend additional time in the chat room after my shift is over. If they feel the need for more information or have more questions, they can contact me by E-mail, but there is a charge for this."

Upsides and Downsides

"I enjoy the work; I enjoy helping people understand that dreams are about ourselves, about issues we are dealing with—either past, present, or future.

"Most times, the people I speak with understand what I am telling them and, after I explain it to them, are able to relate the dream to some area of their lives. I like knowing that many people leave me with a better understanding of what is going on in their lives. I feel good when I can clear up the messages that have come to my clients in a dream state.

"For example, many people have visits from loved ones in their dreams—I always enjoy telling them about this. It is always a pleasure to put a mind to rest after explaining to someone that, yes, this visit was real; your friend or loved one is fine.

"I have found that most people really want to understand themselves. They want to deal with things, not hide them away in a closet. But, there are those who, for whatever reason, simply do not understand. They keep asking the same questions over and over. It's as if they don't like the answer I give them and they think if they ask again maybe it will change.

"And then there are the times when absolutely nothing comes through. It is either because it isn't time for them to have the information yet, it isn't my place to tell them, or they are making up the dream—and, yes, this does happen."

Salaries

"The on-line work is volunteer. I charge $30 per dream through mail. The client mails me the check, and once it clears, I do the interpretation. But, I am not in this for the money. I do this because I was led to do it. It is my way of giving back to the universe, a way of saying thank you for all my blessings."

Advice from SuZane Cole

"Be honest. If you choose to use your gift, always use it in the highest regard. Don't let it come from your ego—ego has no place here. Always give thanks—thanks to your guides and to the universe—and trust your guides; they will lead you."

For More Information

Association for Astrological Networking (AFAN)
8306 Wilshire Boulevard, Suite 537
Beverly Hills, CA 90211
www.afan.org

AFAN is a network linking and informing the international astrological community. AFAN publishes a newsletter and organizes conferences.

Astrological Association of Great Britain (AAGB)
Unit 168, Lee Valley Technopark
Tottenham Hale
London N17 9LN
Great Britain
www.astrologer.com/aanet/welco.html

The AAGB has approximately sixteen hundred members around the world and produces four publications—the *Journal,* published six times a year; *Correlation*, an academic biannual journal on astrological research; a newsletter containing information, debate, and opinion; and the *Medical Astrology Newsletter*, the only journal in the world devoted to medical astrology. The AAGB also organizes occasional seminars on all aspects of astrology, as well as an annual conference.

International Society for Astrological Research (ISAR)
P.O. Box 38613
Los Angeles, CA 90038
www.isarastrology.com

ISAR provides members with its journal, the *International Astrologer*, mailed quarterly. Other benefits of membership include reduced admission to conferences; a subscription to *UAC*, a weekly E-mail newsletter; and a free biennial membership directory.

CHAPTER THREE

The Mind

Careers in Spiritual Health

Although "Star Trek" proclaimed that space was the final frontier, scientists firmly believe the mind is. Some liken it to a muscle that, if not used, will atrophy. Others are convinced we possess psychic powers not yet fully explored (see Chapter 2); and still others feel that attending to the mind as well as the body (see Chapter 4) is the only way to complete spiritual, emotional, psychological, and physical health.

Those who choose professions devoted to the mind and our spiritual life fill traditional as well as nontraditional (New Age) careers. But some cannot really be separated into two distinct mind and body categories. For example, psychiatrists attend to emotional problems but often prescribe drugs to create an effect on the body to accomplish their goals. The hypnotherapist helping someone to recover from an addiction approaches the physical problem through mental processes. The yoga therapist, while concerned with attitude and mood, works predominately with muscles and physical exercise. For most of these professions, the practitioner takes a holistic approach, treating the mind as well as the body.

For the purposes of this book, those professions that focus on the mind or approach the body through the mind are covered in this chapter; those that focus mainly on the body are covered in Chapter 4.

But first, let me offer a disclaimer. The job titles mentioned in this chapter, for the most part, fall into the realm of traditional. There are a slew of therapies and the therapists who provide them that fall into what is known as New Age. But to many people, these New Age therapies are considered bogus, the practitioners who work with them nothing more than quacks, the clients who participate nothing short of victims.

As in any profession, there are schemers and charlatans and people who do not have the best interests of their clients in mind. This seems a concept so foreign to what New Age stands for, but it is still true.

In no other areas than those dealing with the mind and body are traditional and New Age practitioners more at odds with each other. There are scientists and traditional therapists who believe that New Age therapies don't really work, that the therapist presses his or her belief system onto the client, and that the client, motivated to feel better, unconsciously adopts the therapist's belief system.

Therapy in the hands of the wrong people can be a dangerous tool. Traditional psychologists, counselors, and the like must go through years of training and internships and must meet governing body requirements to be licensed to practice. Anyone can hang out a shingle and pin on a job title. No one is there to police them; no one is there to warn patients that the so-called therapist has no actual training.

Know Thyself

Because most future therapists undertake therapy themselves—to know themselves—there are those reading this book who might pursue certain therapeutic avenues without knowing whether or not they are in good hands.

Although the title *Crazy Therapies: What Are They? Do They Work?* sounds more disparaging than the content, this is a must-read for any open-minded future therapist to see both sides of the coin. The book was coauthored by Margaret Thaler Singer and Janja Lalich and published by Jossey-Bass in 1996 in San Francisco. Margaret Thaler Singer has been a clinical psychologist, researcher, and teacher for more than fifty years. She is currently an emeritus adjunct professor of psychology at the University of California, Berkeley. For the past twenty years, she has also done work on cults and is considered an expert in the field of cult menaces. Janja Lalich is an educator, author, and consultant in the field of cults and psychological persuasion.

According to a thorough and entertaining book review by Dr. Robert Carroll, a professor of philosophy at Sacramento City College, the "crazy" therapies examined all claim to be miracle cures and to work like magic. All except facilitated communication claim that their one approach will work for just about everybody, no matter what the problem or situation. "It is unlikely that all these cookie-cutter theories—one size fits all—are correct," says Carroll, "but none of their practitioners seem interested in any scientific studies that might prove once and for all which theory, if any, is correct. . . .

"Singer and Lalich discuss the origins and dangers of each of these 'crazy' therapies. One thing they all have in common is that they have not been proven effective by any independent scientific studies, nor are they generally accepted as effective in the scientific community. Their support comes mainly from the 'insight' and observations of their founders, and patient feedback which is analyzed and evaluated by the therapists themselves. Most of the innovative therapists reviewed by Singer and Lalich seem uninterested in scientifically testing their theories, though most seem attached to technical jargon."

The full review of this book was originally published on the Web at www.skepdic.com/refuge/crazy.html. *Crazy Therapies* can be ordered through any traditional or on-line bookstore.

Possible Job Titles

The realms of counseling and therapy and attending to our spiritual lives are looked at in this chapter. Possible job titles include:

- Counselor

- Minister

- Pastor

- Psychologist

- Hypnotherapist

- Therapist

Under each main title can fall many specializations or subcat-egories. For example, under *counselor*, we could find *career counselor, marriage counselor, guidance counselor*, and so on. Psychologists have specializations such as school psychology, child psychology, counseling, social work, clinical psychology, and more.

Here we look at two main paths: therapists, as an umbrella term for counselors and psychologists, and the ministry.

Therapists

Now it's time for another disclaimer. Perhaps there are a lot of "crazy" therapies out there, but there is a lot of middle ground, too, with nontraditional therapy that is nurturing and that helps the client toward self-awareness and personal growth.

With all that in mind, let's take a closer look at three differ-ent therapies: hypnotherapy, traditional psychotherapy as per-formed by trained and licensed psychologists, and counseling.

Hypnotherapy

Even though Carroll's article states that there are no governing bodies for hypnotists/hypnotherapists, several professional associations do exist. The American Council of Hypnotist Examiners (ACHE) is the primary hypnotherapy certification agency in the United States, with nearly ten thousand members. It was not the first hypnotist organization, but it was the first to initiate registration, certification, and significant educational requirements for its members. It is the only major hypnotherapist certifying organization in the United States that requires its approved schools are state licensed as required by law. Its address is provided at the end of this chapter.

Many other organizations with impressive-sounding names have in recent years claimed to offer certification. The ACHE feels that the vast majority have damaged the profession by approving illegal programs and schools, thus seeming to give them legitimacy.

If you're interested in pursuing training in hypnotherapy, the ACHE advises that you especially avoid any illegal (not state-licensed) schools and schools that claim any form of certification for less than 150 hours of classroom instruction.

What Is Hypnotherapy?

Hypnosis is a state of focused awareness. Hypnotherapy is a technique that uses hypnosis to access the subconscious mind. Hypnotherapists can learn safe and effective ways to induce hypnosis and utilize many forms of hypnotherapy to help clients stop smoking, lose weight, deal with pain, and achieve overall wellness.

Training in hypnotherapy can be for a career on its own or as an adjunct to another therapeutic specialty. One example of using hypnotherapy as a career on its own would be a certified hypnotherapist trained to work in harmony with local health care professionals to aid individuals in dealing with specific medical challenges and procedures. The goal is to reduce the stress the individual is experiencing as a hospital patient and/or surgical or dental patient.

Psychotherapy

Psychologists in applied fields counsel and provide mental health services in hospitals, clinics, or private settings. They can also work in other unrelated areas to the therapeutic setting and, for example, conduct training programs or market research.

Because psychology deals with human behavior, psychologists apply their knowledge and techniques to a wide range of endeavors, including human services, management, education, law, and sports.

In addition to the variety of work settings, psychologists specialize in many different areas.

Clinical psychologists, who constitute the largest specialty, generally work in independent or group practice or in hospitals or clinics. They may help the mentally or emotionally disturbed adjust to life and are increasingly helping all kinds of medical and surgical patients deal with their illnesses or injuries. They may work in physical medicine and rehabilitation settings, treating patients with spinal cord injuries, chronic pain or illness, stroke, arthritis, and neurologic conditions, such as multiple sclerosis. Others help people cope with life stresses such as divorce or aging.

Clinical psychologists interview patients; give diagnostic tests; provide individual, family, and group psychotherapy; and design and implement behavior modification programs. They may collaborate with physicians and other specialists in developing treatment programs and help patients understand and comply with the prescribed treatment.

Some clinical psychologists work in universities, where they train graduate students in the delivery of mental health and behavioral medicine services. Others administer community mental health programs.

Counseling psychologists perform many of the same functions as clinical psychologists. They use several techniques, including interviewing and testing, to advise people on how to cope with problems of everyday living, whether personal, social, educational, or vocational.

Health psychologists promote good health through health maintenance counseling programs that are designed, for example, to help people stop smoking or lose weight.

Training

A doctoral degree is usually required for employment as a licensed clinical or counseling psychologist. Psychologists with a Ph.D. qualify for a wide range of teaching, research, clinical, and counseling positions in universities, elementary and secondary schools, private industry, and government. Psychologists with a Doctor of Psychology (Psy.D.) degree usually work in clinical positions. An Educational Specialist (Ed.S.) degree will qualify an individual to work as a school psychologist. People with a master's degree in psychology may work as industrial-organizational psychologists. Others work as psychological assistants, under the supervision of doctoral-level psychologists, and provide therapy to clients or conduct research or psychological evaluations.

A bachelor's degree in psychology qualifies a person to assist psychologists and other professionals in community mental health centers, vocational rehabilitation offices, and correctional programs. Without additional academic training, opportunities in psychology at the bachelor's level are severely limited.

The American Psychological Association (APA) presently accredits doctoral training programs in clinical, counseling, and school psychology. Psychologists in independent practice or those who offer any type of patient care, including clinical, counseling, and school psychologists, must meet certification or licensing requirements in all states and the District of Columbia. Licensing laws vary by state and by type of position.

Aspiring psychologists who are interested in direct patient care must be emotionally stable, mature, and able to work effectively with people. Sensitivity, compassion, and the ability to lead and inspire others are particularly important qualities for clinical work and counseling.

Salaries

Last year the Bureau of Labor Statistics reported that the median annual earnings of salaried psychologists were $48,050. The middle 50 percent earned between $36,570 and $70,870 a year. The lowest 10 percent earned less than $27,960 and the highest 10 percent earned more than $88,280 a year.

Median annual earnings in the industries employing the largest number of psychologists are as follows:

Offices of other health care practitioners	$54,000
Hospitals	$49,300
Elementary and secondary schools	$47,400
State government, except education and hospitals	$41,600
Other health and allied services	$38,900

The federal government recognizes education and experience in certifying applicants for entry-level positions. In general, the starting salary for psychologists having a bachelor's degree was about $20,600 in 1999; those with superior academic records could begin at $25,500. Psychologists with a master's degree and one year of experience could start at $31,200.

Psychologists with a Ph.D. or Psy.D. degree and one year of internship could start at $37,800, and some individuals with experience could start at $45,200. Beginning salaries were slightly higher in selected areas of the country where the prevailing local pay level was higher. The average annual salary for all psychologists in the federal government was $66,800 in 1999.

Counseling

Counselors assist people with personal, family, educational, mental health, and career decisions and problems. Their duties depend on the individuals they serve and the settings in which they work.

School and college counselors—in elementary, secondary, and postsecondary schools—help students evaluate their abilities, interests, talents, and personality characteristics to develop realistic academic and career goals.

They operate career information centers and career education programs. High school counselors advise on college majors, admission requirements, entrance exams, and financial aid and on trade, technical school, and apprenticeship programs. They help students develop job search skills such as resume writing and interviewing techniques. College career planning and placement counselors assist alumni or students with career development and job hunting techniques.

Elementary school counselors observe younger children during classroom and play activities and confer with their teachers and parents to evaluate their strengths, problems, or special needs. They also help students develop good study habits. They do less vocational and academic counseling than secondary school counselors.

School counselors at all levels help students understand and correct their social, behavioral, and personal problems. They emphasize preventive and developmental counseling to provide students with the life skills needed to prevent problems before they occur and to enhance personal, social, and academic growth.

School counselors provide special services, including alcohol- and drug-abuse prevention programs and classes that teach students to handle conflicts without resorting to violence. Counselors also try to identify cases involving domestic abuse and other family problems that can affect a student's development.

Counselors work with students individually, in small groups, or with entire classes. They consult and work with parents, teachers, school administrators, school psychologists, school nurses, and social workers.

Rehabilitation counselors help people with the personal, social, and vocational effects of disabilities.

Employment or vocational counselors help individuals make career decisions.

Mental health counselors emphasize prevention and work with individuals and groups to promote optimum mental health. They help individuals overcome addictions and substance abuse, suicide, stress management, problems with self-esteem, issues associated with aging, job and career concerns, educational decisions, and issues of mental and emotional health as well as family, parenting, and marital problems.

Mental health counselors work closely with other mental health specialists, including psychiatrists, psychologists, clinical social workers, psychiatric nurses, and school counselors.

Other counseling specialties include marriage and family, multicultural, or gerontological counseling. A *gerontological counselor* provides services to elderly persons who face changing lifestyles because of health problems and helps families cope with these changes. A *multicultural counselor* helps employers adjust to an increasingly diverse workforce.

Training

Formal education is necessary to gain employment as a counselor. About six out of ten counselors have master's degrees. Fields of study include college student affairs, elementary or secondary school counseling, education, gerontological counseling, marriage and family counseling, substance abuse counseling, rehabilitation counseling, agency or community counseling, clinical mental health counseling, counseling psychology, career counseling, and related fields.

Graduate-level counselor education programs in colleges and universities usually are in departments of education or psychology. In 1999, 133 institutions offered programs in counselor education—including career, community, gerontological, mental health, school, student affairs, and marriage and family counseling—that were accredited by the Council for Accreditation of Counseling and Related Educational Programs (CACREP).

Another organization, the Council on Rehabilitation Education (CORE), accredits graduate programs in rehabilitation counseling. Accredited master's degree programs include a minimum of two years of full-time study, including six hundred hours of supervised clinical internship experience.

In 1999, forty-five states and the District of Columbia had some form of counselor credentialing, licensure, certification, or registry legislation governing practice outside schools. Requirements vary from state to state. In some states, credentialing is mandatory; in others, it is voluntary.

Clinical mental health counselors usually have master's degrees in mental health counseling, another area of counseling, or in psychology or social work. Voluntary certification is available through the National Board for Certified Counselors, Inc. Generally, to receive certification as a clinical mental health counselor, a counselor must have a master's degree in counseling, two years of post-master's experience, a period of supervised clinical experience, a taped sample of clinical work, and a passing grade on a written examination.

Salaries

Self-employed counselors who have well-established practices, as well as counselors employed in group practices, usually have the highest earnings, as do some counselors working for private firms, such as insurance companies and private rehabilitation companies.

Median annual earnings of vocational and educational counselors in 1998 were $38,650. The middle 50 percent earned between $28,400 and $49,960. The lowest 10 percent earned less than $21,230, and the highest 10 percent earned more than $73,920. Median annual earnings in the industries employing the largest numbers of vocational and educational counselors are shown below:

Elementary and secondary schools	$42,100
State government, except education and hospitals	$35,800
Colleges and universities	$34,700
Job training and related services	$24,100
Individual and family services	$22,300

The Ministry

In an age—a New Age—in which people are questioning and seeking all kinds of information, some people are no longer willing to accept the dogma of the masses. They have turned away from traditional churches and have embraced the beliefs of metaphysical or New Age churches.

According to Rev. Jennifer Baltz (read her firsthand account later in this chapter), the difference between metaphysical or New Age churches and traditional Christian ones is this: "For the most part, metaphysical churches are more open-minded, believe in reincarnation, and also believe that we have the ability to do some of the things Jesus did. In other words, that we are not saved by Jesus' death and rebirth but rather that we are able to follow in his footsteps and do as he taught and practiced. 'And greater works than these shall ye also do.'"

Those who choose to become ministers can either work as freelancers or be employed through the auspices of an organized church. Freelancers can specialize in one particular area, such as spiritual healing, or can generalize, offering a range of services, from conducting rites of passage to leading drum circles.

Ministers affiliated with a church usually must be generalists, working with parishioners in a variety of capacities—as a spiritual counselor or healer or even officiating at weddings. To become a minister, your search will take you to a church whose practices and beliefs match your own. Each church has its own requirements, and many even have their own divinity schools.

Firsthand Accounts

Cheryl-Lani Branson, Therapist/ Career Counselor

Cheryl-Lani Branson has worked as a therapist, career counselor, social worker, and client advocate. She earned her bachelor of arts in English literature with honors in 1975 from the University of Hartford. She also earned two master's degrees. The first is a master of science degree in counselor education, and the second is a master of social work, with a concentration in group work.

She has also participated in numerous workshops and training sessions including:

Science and Consciousness Conference

Bodywise—Newton Learning Systems

Life Balancing—healing system

Temenos (Accessing the Spirit Workshop)

Women's Mysteries Workshop

Voice Dialogue Training (personality subtype)

Pathways to the Psyche (which included ten days in the desert, four in silence and fasting, learning dream interpretation, tarot, symbols, and utilizing different healing methodologies)

Getting Started

"In 1978, I had an ovarian cyst. I went to a physician who suggested that if I ate differently, such as eliminating meat and caffeine and the like from my diet, that I might be able to get the cyst to drain out instead of surgery. Although I ended up having surgery, that was the time that began my awareness of nontraditional ways of healing.

"When I began to take awareness workshops, I realized that there were energies that we couldn't see or feel but existed around us. It's like going into a room and immediately having a reaction to someone, not based on their looks or the other senses, but based on a vibration or energy that comes off of them. And it is not transference or projection I am talking about; it's an energy field.

"When I finished graduate school the first time, I didn't want to be a guidance counselor, which was the traditional path for people getting a master's in counselor education. I wanted to work in corporate training, which I was able to do. I also noticed that I had an excellent facility for counseling individuals about their careers, and so I began a career-counseling practice at the same time. It was during this private practice that I began to utilize New Age practices.

"To me, New Age is work that is on the cusp, with much of the work based on energy systems. I think the majority of the population has a hard time comprehending what New Age is at first, but with the right exposure, they can slowly come to understand it. Much of the work that is considered New Age is simply an alternate form of healing.

"A lot of my work with clients is not something I learned at workshops but rather through a lot of reading and experiencing. I think the best way to learn New Age methods is to experience them and to surround yourself with people who are open to energy work.

"I have been counseling in one form or another for the past twenty years. As a therapist, I use whatever tools will help the client. My job is to utilize my intuition as well as practical tools for supporting people.

"When I worked as a career counselor, it was in private practice, working with both individuals and groups. I would see the individual clients in an office, but the groups could take place anywhere—in a classroom, in an office, and even outside beside a lake."

What the Work Is Like

"I think it is a blessing for anyone to be able to use New Age techniques in a job or career. In my case, the work I've done has generally been counseling, but I've even been able to use some New Age practices in work I've done as an administrator of training programs. When I've had to deal with negative energy as part of a management team, I've directed rays of light and love through my heart to whomever was being negative. I've sometimes also used that healing light to assist a client in finding closure on some part of his or her life.

"New Age techniques have been especially helpful in my career counseling practice. Nearly every individual client I ever had was 'stuck', and my prescription was to get in water, near water, get water in them. Water creates flow.

"At my last large consulting job I was able to utilize a variety of techniques, including meditation, visualization, manifesting (through treasure maps), and many other healing methods.

"My counseling these days is done with my heart sending love and staying open while we work. Sometimes it's hard to keep my heart open, and I need to remind myself.

"It's very important with this work to revitalize oneself, so I have a number of practices that support me, including yoga, hiking in the mountains (to be awed by the beauty on this earth and reminded of a greater spirit than what is physical), and every once in a while, meditating.

"I often use New Age tools to support myself—I have seven kinds of tarot decks that I use to divine information about a situation. Lately, I pulled runes every night for five days to assist me in determining if it was time for me to leave a work situation. The runes told me to sever, allow myself to change, and then to be still and trust while awaiting the next job opportunity. (Runes are Viking symbols, thousands of years old, used as divination tools.)"

Upsides and Downsides

"There are no downsides to this work—every challenge is just a lesson, either a new one or an old one that one needs reminding of. I feel blessed to be living at this time, when this work is being more accepted. I can use New Age techniques whether I'm working as a counselor, an administrator, or a business consultant. And I am paid to have my heart be open and to learn!"

Salaries

"I've been consulting for a long time, so my fees have a wide range—anywhere from $20 to $75 an hour. It very much depends on what the tasks are.

"A person just starting out, if grounded in some practical physical work aside from the New Age work, could probably charge about $35 an hour. It's all about listening to the voice inside—

intuition—and getting guidance from that in relation to the kind of work to do and the fees to charge."

Advice from Cheryl-Lani Branson

"Do the work! Utilize New Age techniques in healing yourself, and after a while, if you're spirited to do so, you will begin to want to share this work with others.

"If you're a person who is set in your ways, pessimistic, or close minded, New Age work is not for you. On the other hand, if you are open to the nonphysical realms and energy work, you may just be a healer waiting to emerge.

"Follow your path. Listen to your intuition. Don't dismiss anything New Age. Experience everything you can. Know that spending your money taking workshops and having sessions with people will return to you multiplied. Trust that you are where you're supposed to be. Be open to the education you are receiving as you do your own healing. If you don't read any books, take any workshops, or see any New Age counselors, just keep an open heart."

Rev. Jennifer Baltz, Minister, Spiritual Teacher, and Counselor

Rev. Jennifer Baltz lives and works in Northern California in the Sonoma County wine country. She is affiliated with the Church of Aesclepion Healing in Marin, California, and works out of her home, offering spiritual counseling and classes, officiating at weddings and other ceremonies, and managing her website, www.creativespirit.com, "a sanctuary for spirit on the Web."

Her education and training include: a B.S. in business from Santa Clara University; clairvoyant, minister's, and teacher's training programs at the Church of Divine Man Seminary, Berkeley (Berkeley Psychic Institute); and healing, spiritual

midwifery, and trancemediumship training at the Church of
Aesclepion Healing in Marin.

Getting Started

"I've been attracted to religion and spirituality since I was a little girl. I always had ideas different from many Christians—I
never believed in hell, for instance, and I remembered past life
experiences before I ever knew of the concept of past lives.

"I began taking psychic classes with a visiting British medium
in San Jose. She told me I needed to work on judgment and neu-
trality (which was very true) and that I would eventually find the
right teacher and do this kind of work myself one day.

"Of course I didn't believe her. But a few years later, I was
working at United Way in fund-raising, when I discovered that
the marketing director had an interesting history—he was also a
minister and a psychic teacher. Intrigued, I started taking classes
at his church, graduated as a minister myself, and eventually
ended up working there as assistant to the bishop.

"The clairvoyant, minister's training, and teacher's programs
are all now required to become licensed—that's about three
years or so. When I went through, it was only the clairvoyant
program that was required, but I did the rest anyway. In the
teacher's program, you learn how to teach meditation, intuition,
and spiritual healing, and how to set the crown chakra, respond
to questions and energy from students, and set the energy for a
class. As I gained more confidence and graduated from the
teacher's program, I began teaching meditation and intuition
classes and offering spiritual counseling."

What the Work Is Like

"As a minister, I offer spiritual counseling and teach classes
according to the tenets of my church. We humans are both physical body and immortal spirit. Too often we validate and recog-

nize the physical achievements and looks of a person rather than who he or she is inside as an immortal soul, on a spiritual path of growth and evolution this lifetime. So what I do, in individual counseling, classes, and in my writing, is to say hello to the spirit part—the divine within all of us—and help people reconnect with that part of themselves.

"Intuition is really just being in good communication with your soul, with God, and that is what I try to help people do. When you are in touch with your soul essence, you have much greater certainty about who you are, why you are here, and what you really want (as opposed to what everyone else wants for you). So it's both about having a happier life this time around and also about creating real growth and evolution as spirit.

"I think New Age is a very well-used term, but in essence, it is about bringing an understanding and awareness of spirit and spirituality into everyday life.

"At present, I teach classes by phone to people from all over the country. I also offer intuitive spiritual counseling to people in life transitions.

"I work mostly from home. It's very quiet and peaceful, and I usually spend my day doing spiritual counseling, writing class curricula and messages, and updating my website, where everything is posted.

"I have time to garden. Sometimes I attend local spiritual functions, and some evenings, I teach classes. I teach many classes by telephone, since many of my students live in other states. I'm working on some on-line classes, too."

Upsides and Downsides

"The upside is that I can create my day as I choose and I am not working in a corporate environment. I also have time for writing, which I like to do in my spare time. The downside is that I am home a lot and that I must stay focused to get everything done.

"I am always working—usually seven days a week, part-time each day—and it is very difficult to get away for vacations. Also, sometimes people call in crisis at dinnertime!"

Salaries

"I charge different fees and honoraria, depending on what I'm doing. For classes, it is usually about $15 for a one-hour class or $60 for four weeks. For spiritual counseling, it is generally between $50 to $90 per session, and for weddings, usually around $250.

"If you are just starting out as a spiritual teacher, you can expect to charge similar rates for classes—or more if you are teaching longer sessions. Local evening classes can be $25 per person, and weekend seminars can be $50 to $80 per day. I like to keep things reasonable for most people. Weddings depend on the area and the going rate among local clergy."

Advice from Rev. Jennifer Baltz

"As a spiritual teacher, you must maintain your boundaries and your center. To do this kind of work, it is important to have spiritual tools that you can use to stay grounded, to keep your certainty. In a sense, you have to keep one foot in the 'real world' and one foot in the spiritual realm—crossing over from one to the other as an intermediary.

"Your students need for you to be a Rock of Gibraltar, and it is important to have self-care practices that allow this. It is important to take care of yourself, otherwise you can start taking on the problems of other people. So, you must have some form of exercise, some kind of physical work to keep you grounded, and you must know how to separate your energy from the people you work with.

"I think to do this kind of work without taking on negative energies, it is important to have a generally positive attitude about life and a willingness to see things from an innocent per-spective. You must be willing to allow other people to succeed and grow in ways that perhaps you have not achieved yourself, and you must try to be as neutral as you can when handling charged situations.

"You must be committed to your own spiritual growth and evolution and try to live your life and conduct yourself in a way that promotes your evolution and sets a good example for your students. This doesn't mean that you have to be perfect—but be honest and real with people.

"You also need to have good business sense to work on your own. Most people I know who do this kind of work, teaching and counseling, are just scraping by. Why? They are not business savvy, and they don't know how to negotiate for things and ensure that their activities generate income.

"Income varies tremendously, depending on how real you are with people, whether or not you 'walk your talk,' and on your ability with money. It is income minus expenses, so you have to keep a rein on the expenses. A lot of spiritual people don't know how to do that. If you don't have this ability naturally, you need to go back to school. Your local junior college is a great inex-pensive place to pick up some business classes.

"It takes two to three years to build up a reputation and clien-tele enough to do this independently and make a living with it. It is a lot of hard work, but it is also incredibly rewarding."

Rev. Paula Cooper, Spiritual Counselor

Rev. Paula Cooper works from a home office in upstate New York as a spiritual counselor. She earned a doctor of divinity from the Institute of Holistic Theology in Youngstown, Ohio.

She is an ordained minister and also has an extensive back-ground as director of patient services for a four-facility radiation oncology center.

Getting Started

"When I was seventeen, my favorite aunt died of a cerebral hem-orrhage right in front of me. She had been deteriorating for two weeks, and I had been praying for two weeks that she would live, that she wouldn't leave me. As she worsened, she fell into a coma. Her breathing was labored and sporadic; she was losing weight rapidly. One day, as I stood beside her hospital bed, I real-ized she wouldn't want to keep on living like that, and I was able to let go of my selfish desire of wanting to keep her with me and instead turn her fate to God. I went into the hall, and I prayed to God to help her stop suffering. Within moments, I heard her breathing change to what some people call the death rattle. Her body was making desperate attempts to draw air into her fluid-filled lungs. I stepped back into the room and stood with her while she died. For a long time afterward, I was angry with God for not answering my prayers to save my aunt, until I real-ized that God does answer all prayers, but sometimes the answer is no.

"As I grew older and learned more about God and prayer, I began to long to help others understand that even if God says no, God still exists and still loves them.

"I also want to help others understand how God's love and miracles manifest in many small, subtle ways every day and that sometimes 'healing' does not mean 'cure' but instead means acceptance and adaptation. But most of all, I wanted to help oth-ers return to their own divinity and to know that—no matter what—God is there, waiting to love them.

"Due to my strong belief that one's spiritual progression can-not and should not be mandated by any institution (govern-mental, religious, or educational), I pursued my training via nontraditional methods. I have devoted the past twenty-five years to the study of comparative religion, philosophy, Eastern thought, psychology, metaphysics, and the physical sciences (just to name a few!) through self-study, directed study with various independent teachers and spiritual guides, auditing of college classes, as well as through my own independently directed research.

"I got my first job in a people-services field with a cancer treatment group for whom I had already been working. When the physicians wanted to improve their group's standing among the competition with other treatment centers, I suggested and was hired to develop and direct the Patient Support Services Center, which offers emotional support, coordinates volunteers to provide rides to and from therapy, and works with social service agencies in the area to find the patients whatever assistance they might require."

What the Work Is Like

"Currently, I am self-employed as a spiritual counselor and educator. There is so much need in our world, and I feel I can serve my clients' spiritual needs best by serving them from a nonaffiliated, interfaith perspective.

"I provide counseling and educational services to help others learn about the power of choice and how to make the right choices for themselves.

"Many people confuse spiritual counseling with pastoral and psychological counseling, but they are all very different. As a spiritual counselor, I work to help people more effectively use faith and religious beliefs in their everyday lives.

"Some spiritual counselors attempt to bring their clients into a state of 'divine perfection,' but I prefer to help my clients do two things—one: accept the unchangeable realities of life and learn to use their divinity to have happy, good lives in spite of them; and two: learn to recognize the aspects of their lives that can be changed and how to utilize their divinity to guide them in the right directions and to give them strength when things get rocky. I teach methods of effective prayer and choice making to accomplish these goals.

"Being self-employed, I do everything from ordering office supplies to providing counseling to fixing the computer when it glitches. Typically, my days are spent researching and preparing the materials I use in my ministry and counseling. This can mean anything from researching how a client's medical illness can affect his or her emotional stability and/or intellectual abilities to designing, writing, and creating a page for my website. I can honestly say I have yet to be bored with my work!

"I work an average of sixty to seventy hours a week. The majority of my work is done through written or electronic media, so I don't spend a lot of time in face-to-face counseling. Most of my time is spent alone with my computer and books and phone. You really need to be a self-starter and somewhat of a loner to enjoy this job. You must like the tedious (and very often frustrating) tasks of research, writing, and software development. At the same time, you must like working with and helping people, and you must possess the ability to be articulate and personable so that you're ready for those face-to-face clients and seminars.

"In face-to-face encounters, you must maintain your distance in the relationship, while balancing that with loving compassion. As in pastoral or psychological counseling, it is unhealthy for both you and the client to develop a personal relationship. Boundaries must be established and protected. Sometimes that's really hard to do because there will be people you will care about on a deeper, personal level, people you will just plain like and wish you could be friends with. You have to keep in mind that if this person were able to talk to a friend and get help from a friend, he or she wouldn't be seeking a spiritual counselor. Once you cross that line from counselor to friend, you've jeopardized the professional relationship."

Upsides and Downsides

"What I like the most is having the opportunity to help others reconnect with their spiritual selves and learn that they truly do have the power to change their lives. It isn't necessarily—or often—easy, but it is truly possible. So few people believe that. They simply don't understand that they possess the power of choice and that choice is all that is really needed to change a life. It's such a great feeling to help others not only open but walk through that door.

"What I like least is that more people give up when things get hard than those who keep going. A lot of people prefer to place blame on others, or on God, rather than accept responsibility for themselves. It can be very discouraging. Sometimes it can feel very lonely, and sometimes you may experience so many failures you feel like not trying anymore. It takes great effort and determination—and faith—not to give up in those moments."

Advice from Rev. Paula Cooper

"Be sure of the religious/spiritual path you want to follow and what you want to do with your ministry. Those of you who want a physical church and who want to perform marriages, baptisms, and so on, should pursue your training through a church-run seminary. If you want to be a Lutheran minister, for example, you can't approach your training as I did, from a nontraditional perspective. You should attend a Lutheran seminary and be educated within their beliefs and teachings. If you want a church, you must learn about church management, which the seminary will teach you. It's not simply about preaching; it's also running a business, and like any business, it requires good management to prosper.

"If you're interested in providing spiritual counseling and/or teaching (such as in seminars or through educational materials) via the 'working for yourself' route, the paths you can choose to follow are endless. You can still pursue a traditional education, but you should take care not to limit your learning, unless that's what you want to do. If you attend a Baptist school, you're going to learn Baptist beliefs, which is great if you're going to be a

Baptist counselor, but not so great if you want to work with people of all faiths or no faith at all.

"In that case, I would heartily recommend a nontraditional education with a strong foundation of independent exploration into all religions and philosophies. Be open-minded. You'd be surprised how many similarities exist among all the world's major religions. Jesus and Buddha would have been great friends! Be willing to admit that your own beliefs and theologies may be inadequate or just plain wrong.

"Also be prepared for failure and be ready to confront rejection. This is going to be one of the toughest fields to break into and earn a living from. Don't give up when it gets tough. You may have to work a full-time job while building your practice or ministry, but you can build it.

"You may even have to work another job after you are established. Even some ministers who are full-time pastors at long-established churches still have to hold down other jobs to support themselves and their families. This profession is truly a labor of love, but the intangible rewards make it all absolutely worthwhile.

"It's very important to take care of yourself emotionally and spiritually. Ministers and spiritual counselors are exposed to many sad, horrific facts of life. It's easy to begin to doubt that God even exists. You will witness not only successes and joys but also pain and tragedies. Actually, you're going to see the pain and tragedy far more often because it's quite rare for a happy person to seek spiritual advice. Be prepared for that. It's heartbreaking and can be soul-shatteringly sad. You will feel depressed and hopeless at times. You will feel angry at times: angry at your clients, angry at yourself for not being able to help them, angry at God. Those are all normal reactions. Build a support system for yourself so that in those times you have someplace or someone to turn to."

For More Information

Counseling

American Counseling Association
5999 Stevenson Avenue
Alexandria, VA 22304
www.counseling.org

American Dance Therapy Association
www.adta.org

American Music Therapy Association
8455 Colesville Road, Suite 1000
Silver Spring, MD 20910
www.musictherapy.org

National Board for Certified Counselors
3 Terrace Way, Suite D
Greensboro, NC 27403
www.nbcc.org

Hypnotherapy American Council of Hypnotists Examiners
700 South Central Avenue
Glendale, CA 91204
www.sonic.net/hypno/ache.html

American Association of Professional Hypnotherapists
AAPH Headquarters
4149-A El Camino Way
Palo Alto, CA 94306
www.aaph.org

American Psychotherapy and Medical Hypnosis Association
www.apmha.com

International Medical and Dental Hypnotherapy Association
International Headquarters
4110 Edgeland, Suite 800
Royal Oak, MI 48073
www.infinityinst.com/index.html

National Board for Certified Clinical Hypnotherapists
1110 Fidler Lane, Suite L1
Silver Spring, MD 20910
www.natboard.com

Ministries

The religion- and spiritual-based professional associations and ministries are too numerous to list here. An Internet search will yield subcategories such as these, with the approximate number of individual websites in parentheses:

- Apologetics (2)

- Canada (20)

- Catholic (141)

- Churches of Christ (1)

- Evangelical (45)

- Evangelistic (13)

- Family (5)

- Humanitarian (72)

- International (25)

- Lutheran (34)

- Ministries (169)

- Missions (252)

- Orthodox (15)

- Prayer (4)

- Professional (8)

- Regional (12)

- Rescue (5)

- Seventh-Day Adventists (11)

- Society of Friends—Quakers (31)

- Student Christian Organizations (302)

- Unique Organizations (19)

- United Church of Christ (6)

- Youth (45)

Psychology

American Psychological Association
Education in Psychology and Accreditation Offices
Education Directorate
750 First Street NE
Washington, DC 20002
www.apa.org

American Association for Marriage and Family Therapy
1133 Fifteenth Street NW, Suite 300
Washington, DC 20005
www.aamft.org

American Association of Psychotherapists, Inc.
Board of Examiners
P.O. Box 140182
Dallas, TX 75214
www.angelfire.com/tx/Membership/index.html

Canadian Psychological Association
151 Slater Street, Suite 205
Ottawa, ON K1P 5H3
Canada
www.cpa.ca

Social Work
National Association of Social Workers
750 First Street NE, Suite 700
Washington, DC 20002

National Network For Social Work Managers, Inc.
6501 North Federal Highway, Suite 5
Boca Raton, FL 33487

Council on Social Work Education
1600 Duke Street
Alexandria, VA 22314

CHAPTER FOUR

The Body

Alternative Healing Arts Careers

Many New Agers have embraced alternative medicine and alternative healing arts over traditional ways. Although fairly new to this country, much of alternative healing methods date back to Eastern arts that have been in practice for thousands of years. And though some have been slow to catch on here, others are fast becoming commonplace.

Health and natural food stores are no longer a rare sight; even small towns have these popular specialty stores with herbs, vitamins, and organically grown food products. (See Chapter 6 for this career option.) Today dieters, smokers, and others struggling with substance abuse might more readily seek out the help of a hypnotherapist, acupuncturist, or acupressurist than in the past.

Pains in your back and shoulders? A neck that stays permanently stiff? Massage therapists abound, with booths set up at conferences or even in the corridors of your neighborhood mall.

In the past thirty years or so, yoga and meditation have become so familiar to us they're now considered more mainstream than alternative. Then there's aromatherapy, an essence for every ailment; reflexology, a point on your foot that affects corresponding body organs; healing with crystals or magnets; herbalism; and more.

Some Possible Job Titles

Below are just a few of the possible job titles for this wide-open New Age career area. Your own search will undoubtedly uncover a variety of subspecializations as well as completely separate job titles.

Acupuncturist

Acupressurist

Aromatherapist

Doctor of Naturopathic Medicine

Herbalist

Horticultural Therapist

Massage Therapist

Reflexologist

Yoga Instructor

In this chapter we examine the following job options and/or provide firsthand accounts from a:

Massage Therapist

Doctor of Naturopathic Medicine

Herbalist

Horticultural Therapist

Yoga Instructor

Massage Therapy

The healing power of massage has been recognized since ancient times. In as early as the fifth century B.C., the Greek physician Hippocrates wrote that doctors should be experienced "in rubbing . . . for rubbing can bind a joint that is too loose, and loosen a joint that is too rigid."

Various forms of massage were also used by ancient Chinese, Egyptians, and Romans. The technique we know today came into being in the late nineteenth century when Swedish gymnast Per Henrik Ling developed the principles of Swedish massage.

Massage is a systematic manual application of pressure to the soft tissue of the body. It encourages healing by promoting the flow of blood, relieving tension, stimulating nerves, and loosening muscles and connective tissue to keep them limber.

There are dozens of specialized massage techniques in use today, including Reiki, reflexology, Rolfing, and shiatsu. However, the most widespread variation builds upon the original basic strokes of Swedish massage.

Other specialized techniques employed for specific purposes include:

- *Neuromuscular massage*, also known as *trigger point therapy*

- *Deep-tissue massage* on areas of the body suffering from chronic muscle tension, especially effective with tense areas such as stiff necks or sore shoulders

- *Sports massage*, a rapidly expanding field popular among both professional athletes and fitness enthusiasts

Training

It's important to make sure you receive proper training and credentials. Membership in the American Massage Therapy Association (AMTA) means you have graduated from a training program approved by the Commission on Massage Training Accreditation/Approval; hold a state license that meets AMTA certification standards; have passed an AMTA membership examination; or have passed the National Certification Examination for Therapeutic Massage and Bodywork.

Licensing of massage therapists is now required in twenty-five states, and an increasing number of states are adopting the

National Certification Exam. A list of accredited training programs is available from the AMTA. (The organization's address is provided at the end of this chapter.) You can also look in the Yellow Pages for a listing of local schools of massage.

Naturopathy

Naturopathy offers a wealth of mostly harmless and possibly helpful approaches to a healthier diet and lifestyle. Many of its tenets, such as a diet high in fruits, vegetables, and whole grains, are now standard recommendations for those hoping to reduce the risk of cancer, heart disease, and obesity. Its noninvasive physical therapy techniques offer significant relief from a variety of muscle and joint complaints.

Be cautious, though, when considering methods to try yourself or to learn to pass on to others. Some recommendations, such as heat treatments and hydrotherapy, for example, may not necessarily be the most effective way to treat an infection. The various detoxifying measures advocated in naturopathy are even more suspect. There is little proof that a toxic buildup can exist to be dealt with, nor proof that even if one did exist, these particular methods would eliminate it.

Naturopathic practitioners include physicians, chiropractors, nutritionists, holistic nurses, massage therapists, and nonmedical personnel. Their approaches to diagnosis and treatment can vary accordingly. Evaluation of diet and lifestyle is considered the most important. Some naturopathic practitioners could also utilize laboratory analysis, allergy testing—a lot of people seem to be allergic to wheat—and x-rays, as well as a physical exam.

Depending upon your illness and the practitioner's ideology, treatment could include any of the following:

- Herbal medicines—herbs or extracts, prescribed as natural alternatives to synthetic medications

- Dietary supplements and restrictions—vitamins, minerals, enzymes, and other foods, recommended as a natural boost to health and resistance; elimination of certain food categories (such as dairy or red meat)

- Physical manipulation—massage, hydrotherapy, application of heat or cold, and exercise

- Stress management—hypnotherapy, biofeedback, counseling, massage, and other means to reduce or eliminate stress and to cope with any damage from that stress

- Detoxifying methods—fasting or enemas

We must now look at how effective naturopathic methods are—and how potentially dangerous. "First, do no harm." This is of the utmost importance. Second, don't rip off your clients. Selling high-priced protein drinks, for example, that have not been proven scientifically to do anything other than add to a person's daily caloric intake should be a practice to avoid.

Most naturopathic practitioners enter into the field with nothing but good intentions. How well naturopathy works depends on the aspect in question. It's no secret that traditional medicine, having ignored nutrition for decades, now preaches low-fat, high-fiber diets to prevent a range of diseases. Traditional physicians are also now giving credence to certain vitamins and herbs such as St. John's Wort for depression or valerian as a sleep aid.

Having said that, other practices have no proven scientific credibility. Traditional medicine pooh-poohs the notion of toxins building up in the body and discredits fasting or excessive consumption of water as particularly helpful. Megadoses of vitamins have shown to be ineffective in most cases and in some cases harmful. If your body ingests more than it needs of an element, it will either eliminate the excess through normal channels—or there could be a toxic reaction. So the treatment purporting to take care of toxins could actually be the cause.

And eliminating food groups can be dangerous, possibly leading to deficiencies that could cause anemia or other conditions.

We must approach with caution any practice outside the norm that has not undergone extensive clinical trials and research.

Training

Doctors of Naturopathic Medicine (N.D.s) have completed four years of graduate-level training at a naturopathic medical college. There are currently three accredited colleges in the United States: Bastyr College in Seattle; National College in Portland, Oregon; and Southwestern College in Tempe, Arizona.

There are only eleven states that license naturopathic physicians. These physicians must pass either a national- or state-level board examination.

There are now only about 1,500 N.D.s practicing in the United States, as compared to the 577,000 M.D.s and D.O.s practicing. However, judging by current enrollment figures in naturopathic medical schools, the number of N.D.s is expected to double within the next few years.

N.D.s often call themselves general practice family physicians (GPs) or primary-care physicians.

For specific details on admission and curriculum, contact the three accredited training programs already mentioned.

Healing with Plants

For thousands of years, people have recognized the healing properties of plants. Before the creation of synthetic medicines, ancient cultures were knowledgeable about each plant's function and how to tap into its strengths.

In modern times in the United States, this discipline has become almost a lost art. But not quite. Those interested in alternative healing arts still recognize the value of plants for healing.

In addition to their aesthetic value and life-sustaining importance as food, plants have always been the basis for curing common and not-so-common ailments. Products derived from plants and the act of working with plants in general provide us with therapeutic and curative powers.

Horticultural Therapy

Any New Age enthusiast who loves plants can tell you that being close to the soil, working with plants or just sitting in a fragrant and colorful spot, has therapeutic value. Horticultural activity has been long known to relieve tension, improve our physical condition, and promote a sense of accomplishment, pride, and well-being.

The earliest physicians in ancient Egypt prescribed walks in the garden for their mentally ill patients. A signer of the Declaration of Independence, physician Benjamin Rush encouraged his psychiatric patients to tend the gardens. In 1879, Pennsylvania's Friends Asylum for the Insane (today renamed Friends Hospital) built the first known greenhouse for use with mentally ill patients. And after World War II, veterans hospitals—with the help of scores of garden-club volunteers—also promoted similar activity for their physically and emotionally disabled patients.

Today, horticultural therapy is an emerging science based on this time-tested art. In 1955, Michigan State University awarded the first undergraduate degree in horticultural therapy, and in 1971, Kansas State University established the first graduate program in the field.

What Is Horticultural Therapy?

Horticultural therapists use activities involving plants and other natural materials to rehabilitate and/or improve a person's social, educational, psychological, and physical adjustment. This particular field could also be considered a form of spiritual therapy.

Therapists work with people who are physically or developmentally disabled, the elderly, drug and alcohol abusers, prisoners, and those who are socially or economically disadvantaged.

Charles A. Lewis of the Morton Arboretum says, "Plants possess life-enhancing qualities that encourage people to respond to them. In a judgmental world, plants are nonthreatening and nondiscriminating. They are living entities that respond directly to the care that is given them, not to the intellectual or physical capacities of the gardener. In short, they provide a benevolent setting in which a person can take the first steps toward confidence."

Horticultural therapists, in addition to utilizing standard gardening routines, also introduce alternative methods that are sensitive to the special needs of patients. This involves building wide paths and gently graded entrances accessible to wheelchairs and constructing raised beds. Tools are also adapted; short handles, for example, work best with wheelchair-bound individuals, long handles for those with weak backs.

Job Outlook

Because of the continued growth of horticultural therapy, the demand for trained therapists has continued to rise. Horticultural therapists find work in rehabilitation hospitals, nursing homes, substance-abuse treatment centers, prisons, botanical gardens, and through inner-city programs.

Finding That Job

Kansas State University in Manhattan, Kansas, maintains a job bank, and the American Horticultural Therapy Association (AHTA) lists any openings they are made aware of. (The AHTA address is provided at the end of this chapter.)

Some positions find their way into the classified ad section of local newspapers, but most horticultural therapists learn about positions through word of mouth—or they create their own.

Often, rehabilitation centers and hospitals and other appropriate settings aren't aware of the benefits of a horticultural therapy program. Enterprising therapists with public relations skills have learned how to convince administrators that their services are needed. Many begin by volunteering their time, working with patients or clients at the hospitals or through a local botanical garden.

Training

Because horticultural therapy is such a young discipline, finding training is not an easy process. Currently, Kansas State University's department of horticulture, forestry, and recreation resources is the only bachelor's and master's degree program offered in horticultural therapy in the United States. Three universities—Herbert H. Lehman College, Texas A&M University, and University of Rhode Island—offer bachelor's degrees in horticulture with options in horticultural therapy. Edmonds Community College awards a two-year associate's degree in horticultural therapy, and various other institutes, such as Massachusetts Bay Community College and Temple University, offer horticultural therapy electives.

There are several routes an aspiring horticultural therapist can take to become qualified. Dr. Richard Mattson, a professor at Kansas State University's program, recommends a four-year course of study that covers several disciplines.

"Originally, our program was narrowly defined in that we were training students to work primarily in psychiatric hospitals with mentally ill patients. We have a much broader definition today of horticultural therapy. It's more universal. We feel that the human benefits of gardening include mental improvement in areas such as self-esteem and stress reduction and generally improving the quality of life. Horticultural therapy is any kind of interaction of people and plants for mutual benefit. So, we work in community gardens or community farmer's markets. Students work in botanical gardens or arboreta, in the public school systems, or within zoo horticulture. They work in vocational training centers or do international placements with the Peace Corps or in horticultural industry.

"Our concept at Kansas State is that the individual must be trained in a multidisciplinary approach," Dr. Mattson explains. "That means you have to cross over some of the traditional barriers that exist between discipline areas. For example, horticulture is one of the disciplines. Horticulture involves the art and science of growing and culturing plant material in intensive or adapted environments. But then, to work effectively with people, the student must be well trained in areas of psychology and sociology and in education. We think all of those are important. There are also supporting areas such as human ecology, which used to be called home economics. But it's a very important field because it deals with the growth and development of family and relationships. Architecture is also important for creating accessible landscapes. Students can also pursue a number of other areas such as speech pathology, communications, computer science, robotics, human anatomy, and muscle movement."

Also through the auspices of Kansas State's program, students spend a six-month internship gaining practical on-the-job training. Students are supervised by registered horticultural therapists in established programs and are placed coast to coast, from Friends Hospital in Philadelphia to the Chicago Botanical Gardens.

But although desirable, a four-year degree is not necessary to find work as a horticultural therapist. "There are different levels of entry into the field," says Dr. Mattson. "In this country, there are a lot of volunteers who belong to garden clubs and master gardener groups taught by the Cooperative Extension Service. There are some programs that train at the associate arts level, for people who don't have the extra time to devote to their training. But I do think that the bachelor's or master's is important. At some time in the future, the entry for many areas of employment in horticultural therapy will be at the graduate level. Horticultural therapy is not just making flower arrangements or planting gardens. We feel that a multidiscipline training will help individuals apply what's best known in all the related fields. A good example is the importance of business and marketing skills. Many horticultural therapy programs today are cost effective; that is, they are self-sufficient. But in order to utilize the valuable products being produced—whether sacks of potatoes from a vegetable garden or flowers or a landscaping service being provided—an individual needs some kind of skills in how to market the product."

The Registration Process

Although not every employer of horticultural therapists requires registration, being a registered therapist greatly increases your chances of landing a good job. Registration provides the individual with recognition as an accomplished therapist and helps to keep the profession's standards high.

There are three levels of registration: the HTT designation is for the technician who has generally gone through a two-year program; the HTR designation is for someone with a bachelor's; and the HTM is for the person with multiple years of experience and a graduate degree.

Becoming a registered horticultural therapist does not require a degree in horticultural therapy. A degree in a related field or a combination of work experience and education can all lead to professional registration. Decisions about registration are reviewed by a committee from the American Horticultural Therapy Association. They follow a point system, awarding points for the number of years of experience, for publications, for attending seminars, for the number of degrees earned, and other related activities.

Herbalism

An old Webster's dictionary from the 1800s defined an herbalist as one involved with the commerce of plants; an herb doctor or root doctor. Today, most people refer to herbalists as those who use or pick herbs for medicine.

Herbalists fall into several different categories.

- Wildcrafters pick herbs that are going to be used for medicinal purposes.

- Farmers who specifically grow herbs for medicine are considered to be herbalists.

- Herbologists, as the suffix implies, are people who study herbs and identify them but don't necessarily use them.

Training

For those seeking training as an herbalist, there are a number of residency programs in the United States. There are also correspondence courses and various lectures, seminars, and workshops held across the country. The American Herbalist Guild publishes an inexpensive directory that lists all the different programs. It is available by writing to them at their address listed at the end of this chapter.

Although herbalism has been practiced pretty much in the same manner for thousands of years, finding recognition through established channels in this country could take another millennium or two, U.S. herbalists believe.

Herbalist Roy Upton (see his firsthand account later in this chapter) says, "There is a monopolistic control of health care in this country. Specialties such as midwifery, which is accepted worldwide, and herbalism, which is also accepted worldwide by other cultures, are not warmly embraced in this country. But that's changing.

"Presently, there are only two mechanisms by which someone can be licensed to practice medicine and utilize herbs in his or her practice. The first is to become licensed as a naturopathic physician. The other way to become licensed to use herbs is as an acupuncturist. Acupuncture is a foundation of Chinese medicine, and herbalism plays a large role in that discipline. But it has to be through a program that teaches herbal medicine. Not all acupuncture programs do."

Jobs with Herbal Product Manufacturers

There are several kinds of jobs available within the herbal product manufacturing industry:

- Research and development of products involves developing formulas and processing techniques.

- Quality control workers ensure that the plants being used are the right plants, that they are not contaminated, and that they have the potency they should have.

- Writers are needed to develop literature describing the products. (See Chapter 5 for careers in writing.)

- Teaching classes increases consumer awareness about the different products. (See Chapter 7 for careers in teaching.)

Pharmacognosy

Pharmacology is the study of medicinal actions of substances in general. Pharmacognosy is the study of medicinal actions of plants and other natural products.

It doesn't cover, as herbalism does, the practice of herbal medicine or the picking of medicinal plants. It is the job of pharmacognosy professionals to pick the product apart and study its constituents.

Roy Upton explains: "Native American herbalists, for example, might not know that a plant contains volatile oils, alkaloids, and polysaccharides. They don't care about that. They know how to use it, how it works, and that's what's important.

"A pharmacognosist would study those elements, though they wouldn't necessarily know how to use them. The end result of their study is to try to develop synthetic drugs from the natural substances.

"Like herbalism, pharmacognosy was sort of an endangered species. At one time, physicians were trained in botany because they needed to know where their medicines came from. But then there was the separation between pharmacy and medicine, and other subspecialties were created, such as pharmacology and pharmacognosy, which kept on studying medicinal plants. As the chemical revolution took place in the 1800s, there was a big push to develop medicines as patentable substances to create a pharmaceutical industry.

"The craft of the herbalist and the pharmacognosist was less valued. Doctors no longer studied botany, and the thrust was to synthesize medicinal plants so they could be standardized to a certain level of activity. The professions almost died. It's only been in the last twenty years that there's been a resurgence."

Firsthand Accounts

James Miller, Yoga Therapist

James Miller is currently twenty-nine years old and has been a practicing yoga therapist and fitness consultant for ten years. He is self-employed and leases space from Synergy Health Center, a holistic health/massage therapy business in downtown Cedar Rapids, Iowa.

James Miller was in the United States Marine Corps, attended Northern Illinois University for three years, and is certified as a personal trainer and in hatha yoga. He is also a STOTT Pilates conditioning mat/reformer instructor.

Getting Started

"Fitness had always been important to me, and even as early as grade school, I can remember spending my money on vitamins and trying to lift weights. I attended a boarding high school, and the luxury of a weight room and plenty of free time started my commitment to working out. Although I wanted a career in writing, I decided to support myself first by taking a position as a sales manager at a local health club.

"When the time came for the trainers in the club to be certified, the owner asked if I would be interested in testing along with them. I scored the highest, even among trainers who had owned personal training companies for years, and was soon ranked the top trainer in the club. Since this didn't make me very popular and my ambitions were still to attend college and launch a writing career, I decided to enlist in the Marine Corps to reap the benefits of the tuition reimbursement programs. Still interested in fitness, I continued working out and training other marines, eventually organizing a small team to compete in the armed forces bodybuilding competition.

"During all of this, I remained a voracious reader, interested in reading mostly philosophical and spiritual books. This inevitably led me to read of yoga and the Eastern methods of fitness, and I was amazed at the depth of wisdom I found. This was philosophical fitness, a search for the complete expression of a human being's potential and a system so complete in itself that it could be adapted to fit even the most deconditioned clients and lead them to perfect health.

"My tour of duty in the marines complete, I opened my own personal training studio and began working with clients. Slowly, I began to use yoga more and more with each new client as I began to understand how powerful a tool it was to evoke change.

"Still interested in writing, I began to publish fitness articles in international magazines. I am currently working on a manuscript titled *Living Powerfully*. This book will attempt to redefine the reasons we exercise in the West, by showing the beauty and meaning behind the Eastern techniques."

What the Work Is Like

"In working with clients, I employ a host of Eastern techniques, from tai chi and hatha yoga to more esoteric forms of bodywork such as kundalini yoga and Thai massage.

"I am also an ACE certified personal trainer. ACE is the American Council on Exercise, and of the many certifying organizations, it is one of the most respected.

"I am also a STOTT Pilates conditioning mat/reformer instructor. Pilates is an exercise discipline founded by Joseph Pilates around the 1930s. It is yoga based, because of his experience in yoga, but would appear to be almost a preventative form of physical therapy for the mind/body connection. It is the current pinnacle of fitness in the Western world and is the trend both in the media and in the gym.

"STOTT conditioning is one take on the body of work written by Joseph Pilates as understood by Moira Stott, a former dancer and now a heavy hitter in the Pilates world. It is by far the most respected approach toward Pilates, for it combines the essence of Pilates with the most up-to-date information in the physical-therapy world.

"Mat certification is the first level; an instructor learns to facilitate classes without any particular machinery. Reformer certification is machine specific—being certified to facilitate exercise on a rather archaic looking machine with a wide variety of possible exercises. (Joseph developed these pieces of equipment while imprisoned in England during World War II; he used only the equipment available in the camp, such as hospital beds—hence the strange-looking equipment.)

"Overall, Pilates certification is more respected among the medical community than personal training or even yoga.

"The freedom of being self-employed allows me to adapt my work schedule to best fit my life. During a typical day, I begin working one-on-one with clients at 7 A.M. and book hourly through 2 P.M. I find that working back-to-back with clients allows me to keep my energy and attention focused on my work and is a more efficient way to earn money.

"After taking a break in the afternoon, I may work on a host of other projects designed to move my career away from working entirely with clients one-on-one and toward one-on-many, such as my upcoming book and my interactive website.

"The beauty of working for yourself is the endless opportunity and the amazing number of ways to expand your business. In the evenings, I usually teach yoga or Pilates classes at local yoga studios and health clubs. This may seem like a busy work schedule, but the things I do to earn a living are the things I am really interested in, so I rarely feel overworked. On the contrary, I usually feel energized. Working with people so intimately provides for almost a social atmosphere, and sometimes it's easy to forget I am doing my job. Clients become friends, and I look forward daily to seeing them develop and progress."

Upsides and Downsides

"The best part of my job is simple. Each and every time I work with clients, I see them at their best, making positive changes in their lives, becoming stronger, more confident and content with their lives. People are happy when they see me, and I rarely deal with the negativity and stress others experience daily in their jobs. Being a positive part of people's lives brings meaning to my own life, and nothing could be more fulfilling.

"I now realize that the reason I enjoy my job so much is because I am simply sharing the knowledge and skills I have learned over the years with other people. No other job could be easier—or a more perfect reflection of me.

"It is difficult, though, to be a fitness consultant/yoga therapist because it is more than a job; it is a life you, too, must lead. That can be challenging. You must practice what you preach, and each day I continue to discipline myself as I travel the path to perfect health. The further you advance in yoga and in fitness, the further you can bring others, and so I am responsible daily for renewing my commitment to the things I believe in."

Salaries

"I charge $45 per hour of yoga therapy/fitness consulting, and I average between thirty and forty hours weekly.

"In addition to this are the classes I teach through local health clubs. They pay between $60 and $80 per class. Beyond this I have income through phone coaching, writing, and occasionally giving motivational talks on fitness and yoga."

Advice from James Miller

"Explore what you really believe about the human body and our individual paths toward self-perfection. You cannot convince other people to evoke positive change in their lives without believing it yourself first. Most likely the things you believe are represented by the way you are living right now, and this will help you decide if you are ready to help others.

"Read constantly. If you have a thirst for knowledge, this will continue to propel your career to new levels year after year. Become qualified by searching out the best available degrees and/or certifications, but continue to learn from yourself.

"The path you take to perfect health is the same path your clients will travel, and you are there to guide them through the same trouble spots that challenged you. And realize that in the end, if your intent is to help others, you will inevitably succeed. Everything else will take care of itself."

Victoria Pospisil, Eastern Healing Arts Practitioner/Licensed Massage Therapist

Victoria Pospisil is co-owner of Embody Health, a group practice in Mt. Vernon, Iowa, that includes several bodyworkers, counselors, a chiropractor, and an acupuncturist.

She has a bachelor's degree in business and English from Cornell College, Iowa, and she received her P.E.H.A. (Practitioner of Eastern Healing Arts) from Windemere School of Eastern Healing Arts in Decorah, Iowa, in 1999. She has also studied Reiki and received her master/teacher level in 1998.

Getting Started

"I began my spiritual journey in 1993 and discovered Reiki, which is a hands-on form of healing. From there my love for working with life-force energy became a passion. This naturally led to studying the Eastern philosophy of energy and traditional Chinese medicine.

"I kept asking in prayer 'How can I serve?' And the more I asked, the more doors opened for me along this path. As I delved further into Reiki and Qigong, I felt as if I were coming home. Friends and family began to seek out my healing sessions, and I knew I needed to be ethical and knowledgeable about my work. I sought out a school that would give me the information I needed."

What the Work Is Like

"Eastern healing arts incorporate the concept of energy in the form of a subtle life force that moves throughout the human body. This life force energy comes in many forms and can be transferred from one person to another.

"My job is to find imbalances within the energy field of a client and, by using various methods, facilitate balance and health. The various methods I use include Tuina, which is

Chinese medical massage, acupressure, shiatsu, or neuromuscular therapy. I always incorporate energy work, such as Reiki or Qigong, in my sessions. This way, I know I am addressing the physical body, but I am also seeking to help the client understand why this imbalance happened in the first place.

"Embody Health is in a small college town with larger cities within close driving range. Our clients are professional people with extra income and an interest in their health.

"My duties include setting up a quiet, comfortable healing environment. This sounds easy, but it is difficult to find all of these in one place. The next task is one of the most challenging parts of my job—staying centered all of the time. I am a mom with two busy teens and a farm. But, I find that when I arrive to work, I can easily move into a place of calm just by using my breath and allowing my mind to empty to receive the 'flow,' which is always available.

"In a typical day, I see about four clients. I allow ninety minutes per person, including time to greet them, talk about what their needs are for the session, give them time to undress and then dress afterwards, and then leave time for post-session communication. The time is barely sufficient, and it's one of my challenges.

"As for the hour they are actually on my mat, or my massage table, it is wonderful! It is just us and quiet music or silence and the intention of our mutual agreement concerning their needs. When you invite the divine into your work, wonderful things happen!"

Upsides and Downsides

"I love my work when I am in the session. I do not like the paperwork that is involved in the massage process as far as insurance companies are concerned. And, unfortunately, the paperwork is required more and more frequently."

Salaries

"I charge $50 per session. I usually work on four clients per day and work five days per week. This is all pretty loose, however, because some people cannot afford the fee, insurance won't cover them, and I am their source of comfort. I do ask for some energy exchange, but it may not always come in the form of money, and sometimes it is my form of tithing to God."

Advice from Victoria Pospisil

"Be prepared to handle the following: inconsistent income, paperwork, clients with their own agendas and timelines, the need to find creative ways to add on extra income, that is, other products to sell with your services.

"Also count on miracles—they are around every corner in the business of service with God.

"In my opinion, the field of energy medicine is virtually in its infancy. We have the benefit of thousands of years of practice from the East, but we have had little ways of measuring how it works or even why it works. This is an exciting field to work in, if this is your passion. This is also a field that has such a high level of gratification to it. To have someone come to you, totally stressed out or suffering from lack of sleep because of physical pain and to have them walk out feeling so much better, that is a great job!

"My advice would be to find a school with an excellent repu-tation for delivering competent, qualified therapists and then begin, knowing you will probably be studying and learning the rest of your life.

"You must be in good physical shape to approach this career, and you must be in excellent mental health, because you need to be well balanced to work with people at this level. There is also a level of organization needed in this field, and there is some paperwork, so these skills are useful. And before you dive in, talk with another massage therapist."

Nancy Stevenson, Horticultural Therapist

Nancy Stevenson has worked as a horticultural therapist for more than twenty years. She earned a bachelor's degree in political science, then later went on for a master's in human services and became registered by the American Horticultural Therapy Association (AHTA).

Getting Started

"I became interested in horticultural therapy in the early seventies when it was still just a fledgling profession. The national organization, AHTA, was founded in 1973. At first I was a volunteer at a boys' detention center, working with someone who had started an indoor gardening program there. My colleague, Libby Reavis, who I've been working with ever since, volunteered with me. We became more and more interested and realized there was a real need in Cleveland to develop some training for this field. We worked through the Garden Center of Greater Cleveland (now known as the Cleveland Botanical Garden) to start some workshops. We stayed as volunteers until 1981. Then Libby and I joined the staff sharing a full-time job between us. We went to them and explained that the job had become too big for us to handle as volunteers. We were spending twenty hours a week apiece on this. If they wanted to get into horticultural therapy in a big way, they needed a paid position. We helped them design the job and set the salary."

What the Work Is Like

"Over the years, we've had quite a varied program through the garden center. We contract with different agencies for outreach programs. Typical programs have been at children's hospitals or nursing homes. We'd go every other week and design a yearlong curriculum that included indoor and outdoor gardening. We have activities that involve repotting or propagation from seeds and cuttings. We work with plants and dried materials for crafts—pressed flowers, flower arranging, and that sort of thing.

"A good 60 percent of our time is spent out in the community. We recently developed a three-year program of intergenerational gardening in a neighborhood center in the inner city. The program brings seniors and elementary school students together.

"We do a lot of public speaking to garden clubs and civic organizations to help educate people about horticultural therapy and its benefits.

"I have also been involved with training future horticultural therapists through the Cleveland Botanical Garden, which offers a six-month internship program."

Salaries

"The American Horticultural Therapy Association conducts an annual survey to determine salary levels for nonregistered therapists, HTTs, HTRs, and HTMs. The average salary of therapists with one year or less of employment experience is around $25,000 per year. Averages go up with the number of years of work experience, but not much. Therapists can expect to earn around $27,000 with one to five years experience, $28,000 with five to ten years experience, and $34,000 with ten or more years. Salaries increase by $1,500 to approximately $2,500 or so per year for those who have obtained professional registration.

"There are a lot of rewards to this profession, but money certainly isn't one of them. I think the reward for me is being able to combine horticulture and gardening, which have always been very strong interests of mine, with working directly with people—helping people learn about the therapeutic benefits of gardening and how working with plants can help them, no matter what their disabilities or limitations are.

"I think the relationship between therapist and client is very important. You set up a nonthreatening situation where positive change can occur for someone. You have to build trust."

Advice from Nancy Stevenson

"The ideal personality for a horticultural therapist is usually someone who's fairly outgoing and comfortable with people and able to express him- or herself well. You should have a natural bent for teaching and be able to communicate with people to instruct them on basic gardening techniques. It's kind of an elusive quality, but you should have whatever that something is that makes people feel comfortable with you, to be able to talk freely with you. It's similar to the qualities most kinds of therapists should possess.

"I think you also have to be able to stay fairly detached and not become too emotionally involved with the people you're trying to help, otherwise it can be hard on you."

Roy Upton, Herbalist

Roy Upton is president of the American Herbalist Guild and an herbalist who, through his writing and lecturing, is involved with teaching people the medicinal value of plants. He writes books and magazine articles and teaches classes across the country. He also works full-time for a manufacturer of medicinal products, where he is responsible for quality control and answering customers' questions.

Getting Started

"I came across my knowledge in an interesting manner. I lived for three and half years on different Native American reservations in Washington, Nevada, and New Mexico, learning about herbs and their uses. I learned about herbs as a process of living. People got sick; the medicine people picked herbs and made teas or poultices. I absorbed what I was seeing and started learning.

"I then spent four years in St. Thomas, Virgin Islands, and studied the Caribbean's ethnobotany—how cultures use plants for medicine.

"There are different herb doctors in the Caribbean; people go to them just like they go to regular doctors here. One of my teachers was too old to gather the plants, so I would do it for her, and then she would tell me what they were used for. I would then comb through all the literature in the libraries, and eventually, while working on a project for the local college in St. Thomas, cataloging the different medicinal plants and setting up medicinal herb gardens, I learned even more.

"From there I traveled to California, where I am currently based, and I entered into a three-year program studying traditional Chinese medicine."

What the Work Is Like

"I consult with people about their health needs and which types of herbs they can use to deal with different types of ailments. However, unless you are licensed, you cannot hang out a shingle and practice medicine in this country, even if in that practice all you are doing is recommending herbal teas.

"Under the FDA, the Federal Food and Drug Administration, you cannot legally dispense a substance for medicinal use unless that substance has been approved by the FDA. If you give garlic to someone, for example, and tell him or her that it can help lower cholesterol levels, you can be arrested for dispensing illicit drugs. Garlic. But we are pushing the system to change.

"If you walk into any nutrition and health store, you'll see rows of bottles and vials holding all the different herbs in their various forms. How do manufacturers and retailers buck the system? In essence, they are selling non-FDA-approved substances, which are therefore considered illegal.

"But the answer is simple. The products are not packaged as medicines; they are called 'foods.' Trained herbalists know what to do with these 'foods.' They are aware of how the popular medications used in this country—aspirins and sedatives, for example—can be substituted safely with common plants.

"Aspirin was originally derived from a plant called meadow-sweet, for example. The Latin name is *spirea*, which is where the word *aspirin* came from. So, if someone has a headache, we would use a natural source, a tea made with meadowsweet.

"With sedatives, there are more than a million prescriptions written for Valium every year, which involves an expensive doctor visit and an expensive prescription, not to mention all the harmful implications. Instead, we would start with something as simple as chamomile tea, which is what Peter Rabbit's mother gave him. Chamomile is a flower that has essential oils. These oils have calming and sedative properties. There are a whole range of calming herbs that get progressively stronger—from chamomile to skullcap to valerian root.

"Herbalists get the message across without resorting to breaking the law. We teach and write books and articles, we lecture and offer apprentice programs, or we work for herbal product manufacturers."

For More Information

American Council on Exercise
P.O. Box 910449
San Diego, CA 92191

Alternative Medicine Association
7909 Southeast Stark Street
Portland, OR 97215

American Association of Naturopathic Physicians
8201 Greensboro Drive, Suite 300
McLean, VA 22102
www.naturopathic.org

American Association of Colleges of Osteopathic Medicine
6110 Executive Boulevard, Suite 405
Rockville, MD 20852

American College of Sports Medicine (ACSM)
P.O. Box 1440
Indianapolis, IN 46206

American Herbalist Guild
Box 1683
Soquel, CA 95073

American Horticultural Therapy Association (AHTA)
362A Christopher Avenue
Gaithersburg, MD 20879

American Massage Therapy Association (AMTA)
820 Davis Street, Suite 100
Evanston, IL 60201

The American Medical Association (AMA)
515 North State Street
Chicago, IL 60610

American Osteopathic Association
142 East Ontario Street
Chicago, IL 60611

Flower Essence Society
P.O. Box 459
Nevada City, CA 95959

Friends of Horticultural Therapy
362A Christopher Avenue
Gaithersburg, MD 20879

Herb Research Foundation
1007 Pearl Street #200
Boulder, CO 80302

International Physical Fitness Association
415 West Court Street
Flint, MI 48503

The Lady Bird Johnson Wildflower Center
4801 LaCrosse Avenue
Austin, TX 78739

Touch Research Institute (TRI)
University of Miami School of Medicine
Coral Gables, FL 33124

Horticultural Therapy Training Programs

Cleveland Botanical Garden
11030 East Boulevard
Cleveland, OH 44106
(Six-month internship program)

Edmonds Community College
20000 Sixty-eighth Avenue West
Lynnwood, WA 98036
(Two-year program in horticultural therapy)

Kansas State University
Department of Horticulture, Forestry and Recreation Resources
Throckmorton Hall
Manhattan, KS 66506
(B.S. and M.S. program in horticultural therapy)

Kansas State University
Division of Continuing Education
226 College Court Building
Manhattan, KS 66506
(Short-term correspondence course)

Herbert H. Lehman College
The City University of New York
250 Bedford Park Boulevard
West Bronx, NY 10468
(B.S. in horticulture with options in horticultural therapy in
    cooperation with the New York Botanical Garden)

Massachusetts Bay Community College
Wellesley, MA 02181
(Horticultural therapy electives)

The New York Botanical Garden
200th Street and Southern Boulevard
Bronx, NY 10458
(Certificate program)

Rockland Community College
Suffern, NY 10901
(Horticultural therapy electives)

Temple University
Department of Landscape Architecture and Horticulture
Ambler, PA 19002
(Horticultural therapy electives)

Tennessee Technological University
School of Agriculture
Box 5034
Cookerville, TN 38505
(Horticultural therapy electives)

Texas A&M University
Department of Horticulture
College Station, TX 77843
(B.S. in horticulture with options in horticultural therapy)

Tulsa Junior College Northeast Campus
Department of Science and Engineering
3727 East Apache
Tulsa, OK 74115
(Horticultural therapy electives)

University of Massachusetts
Department of Plant & Soil Science
Durfee Conservatory, French Hall
Amherst, MA 01002
(Horticultural therapy electives)

University of Rhode Island
Department of Plant Science
Kingston, RI 02881
(B.S. in horticulture with options in horticultural therapy)

Virginia Polytechnic Institute and State University
Department of Horticulture
Blacksburg, VA 24061
(Horticultural therapy electives)

CHAPTER FIVE

New Age Writers
Careers in Print and Cyberspace

For every area of interest, there is a body of knowledge committed to paper—books and articles for magazines, newspapers, journals, and newsletters. There is also the electronic media with megabytes to fill all over the Internet.

New Age writers have a wealth of subject matter to cover—everything from daily and weekly astrology columns to paranormal reporting, self-help, spirituality, and more.

Here is just a small, general sampling of possible book or article topics:

Acupuncture

Aromatherapy

Astrology

Channeling

Crystals

ESP

Feng Shui

Ghosts

Herbology

Horticultural therapy

Hypnotherapy

Massage

Metaphysics

Naturopathic medicine

Numerology

Paranormal healing

Psychic phenomenon

Pyramids

Reflexology

Reiki

Rolfing

Tarot reading

UFOs

Zener Cards

Each of the above topics lends itself to a specific focus or angle. For example, you could write a general article on hypnotherapy, explaining what it is; or you could describe one particular use, such as helping a client to quit smoking; or you could profile a hypnotherapist; or you could take the approach that hypnotherapy doesn't work and why. One topic, several articles. Similarly, when proposing a book project, you can narrow or broaden a topic as needed.

Markets for Articles

There are two major outlets through which you can locate markets for your New Age article—the current *Writer's Market* (Writer's Digest Books), which includes astrology, metaphysical, and New Age among its many categories, and the Internet. Performing a search on the Internet using key words such as *New Age publications* or *New Age magazines* will deliver thousands of sites. The list that follows is not an endorsement but a sampling of what one such search can uncover.

- *Alchemy*—an E-zine reviewing websites covering a wide range of alternative beliefs and systems of thought. www.alchemy2go.com

- *American Spirit Newspaper*—includes articles on spirituality, meditation, psychic awareness, health, prosperity, and relationships. www.celestia.com/SRP

- *Atlantis Rising Online*—provides access to articles from back issues: *Free Energy, Atlantis, Hall of Records, Emerging Archeology, Astrology, Edgar Cayce, Spirituality, New Age, The Millennium.* www.atlantisrising.com

- *Awareness Magazine*—a bimonthly publication that reaches individuals concerned with many issues that involve the environment, holistic health, natural health products, fitness, and personal growth. www.awarenessmag.com

- *Bliss*—a monthly magazine that publishes articles, interviews, inspiring stories, news, vegetarian recipes, and book, music, and movie reviews. www.bliss2000.com

- *Circles of Light*—published weekly, with original articles and columns concerning astrology and metaphysics. www.circlesoflight.com

- *Conscious Creation Journal*—a bimonthly publication on all aspects of reality creation, metaphysics and consciousness. www.consciouscreation.com/journal

- *Four Directions Web-Zine*—an on-line discussion/zine, patterned after the four directions of the Native American medicine wheel, that includes poetry, reflections, and an interactive forum. www.momo2000.com

- *Galactic News*—a visionary site of current projects underway by the Mystic Broadcast Network. www.mysticbroadcast.org/g-news

- *Global Visionary Newsletter*—published by the Earth Rainbow Network. www.spacesbetweenthings.com/jean/hudon.html

- *In Light Times*—on-line and print newspaper dealing with metaphysical subjects, spirituality, astrology, UFOs, alternative health, relationships, and the paranormal. www.inlightimes.com

- *Innerchange Magazine*—North Carolina's leading resource for personal, spiritual, and planetary transformation, this bimonthly publication focuses on the New Age, spirituality, holistic health, and alternative healing. http://innerchangemag.com

- *INSPIRE, SICA: Online Cultural Quarterly*—explores an intensely personal and spiritual creativity across a broad spectrum of cultural endeavor with SICA Virtual Gallery. www.subud-sica.org

- *Lightworks*—the *Monthly Aspectarian* New Age zine, astrology, daily astro-weather forecast, visionary art gallery, daily comics, daily affirmations. www.lightworks.com

- *Living Traditions Online*—an on-line magazine covering spirituality and academia. www.livingtraditions-magazine.com

- *Magical Blend Magazine*—alternative spirituality magazine.
  www.magicalblend.com

- *Mount Shasta Magazine*—quarterly magazine featuring
  teachers in the New Age and alternative health communities.
  www.mountshastamagazine.com

- *New Earth News*—information about the people, places,
  events, and resources that are transforming our world.
  www.newearthnews.com

- *New Frontier*—an on-line magazine with the theme of
  transformation.
  www.newfrontier.com

- *New Millennium Being*—an astrological-based E-zine
  written with novice and non-astrologers in mind.
  www.yogatech.com/nmb

- Oasis TV—a comprehensive New Age portal featuring
  articles on holistic healing, spirituality, metaphysics, the
  environment, and world peace.
  www.oasistv.com

- *Pathways to Enlightenment*—on-line spiritual journal for
  meditation club.
  www.meditationclub.com/index.htm

- *phenomeNEWS*—an on-line New Age magazine.
  www.phenomenews.com

- *Planet Lightworker*—offers a cross-section of New Age
  material.
  www.Planetlightworker.com

- *Rebel Planet*—articles on mysticism, ancient religions,
  goddesses, gods, alchemy, hieroglyphics, magic, astrology,
  tarot, divination, and book reviews.
  www.lunarace.com

- *Romanticside*—articles on how to improve your health, live life more naturally, daily divination in both tarot and astrology, and candle magick.
  www.romanticside.com

- *Seeds of Unfolding*—ideas for spiritual growth and the development of consciousness, including meditation, spiritual exercises, inspirational biographies, and practical applications for daily living.
  www.seedsofunfolding.org

- *Soulful Living*—interactive on-line guide where topics of interest are explored each month with highly regarded experts and authors.
  www.soulfulliving.com

- *Spiritually Fit Webzine*—stories about spiritual experiences in nature and through music.
  www.spirituallyfit.com

- *The Delphi Oracle*—monthly on-line journal for the Omega Foundation, a New Age awareness community to help people improve their lives in positive and exciting ways through channeling, coaching, psychic development, hypnosis programs, and counseling.
  www.users.uswest.net/~omegafdn/delphi.html

- Whole Again Resource Guide—extensive database of New Age on-line publications and resources.
  www.wholeagain.com/welcome.html

You can look through each of the above sites to determine if they accept freelance work and, if they do, what their terms and conditions are. You can also request writers' guidelines via E-mail or by sending a self-addressed, stamped envelope (SASE) through the post office.

The Elements of an Article

Once you've located markets and determined what type of articles the editors prefer, it's time to sit down and write. Although the subject matter can be very different, most articles include many of the same elements.

All the best articles start with an interesting "hook," that first paragraph that grabs the reader's (and the editor's) attention. They use quotes from real people or experts, cite important facts, give examples, and sometimes include amusing anecdotes or experiences.

Some articles have sidebars, additional information that doesn't fit in the body of the article but would be important for readers to know. Examples of sidebars are a list of the signs of the zodiac and the dates they cover; a recipe to accompany a cooking article; or a list of stores where a particular product can be purchased.

The style or tone of the article will vary according to the publication. Some editors prefer chatty pieces that speak directly to the reader; others prefer a more formal voice.

The content, of course, would be specific to that particular publication. Spiritual growth magazines, for example, might include personal experience pieces, interviews with counselors or healers, and self-help pieces.

Some spiritual growth magazines might use only first-person personal experience pieces; others prefer third-person pieces. Some cover only a U.S. readership; others extend to Europe and beyond.

By studying a publication and sending for its writers' guidelines (a simple request with an SASE will quickly have information in the mail to you), you can see the style, word count, focus, and approach the editors prefer.

Getting That First Article Published

Study the Publications

Read as many publications as you can and, in particular, those you would like to write for. Send for sample copies, spend time at the library, or browse through the racks of newsstands. It's never a good idea to send an article to a publication you have never seen before. If you miss the tone or send two thousand words when they can use only one thousand, you might kill your chances for future acceptances.

Send Your Submission: Two Approaches

Once you have decided what you want to write about, there are two ways you can proceed. You can write the entire article on speculation, send it off to appropriate editors, and hope they like your topic. "On spec" writing is akin to a shotgun approach—fire out a lot of articles and see which ones hit the target. It can be time-consuming and will not necessarily pay off, but new writers usually have no choice—they have to write on spec before they establish themselves. Editors are often unwilling to make assignments to unpublished writers. They want to be sure you can deliver a professional, polished manuscript on time.

The second approach is to write a query letter, a miniproposal, to see if there is any interest in your idea first. Query letters will save you the time of writing articles you might have difficulty selling. Only once you're given a definite assignment do you then proceed.

The Elements of a Query Letter

The best queries are one page in length (single-spaced) and start with a hook—perhaps the first paragraph of your article—to grab the editor's attention. The hook is the focus of your piece, the slant that makes it different from all the other articles out there. In the body of your query letter, you explain your rationale for the piece and your approach—whether you'll be using expert quotes or not, for example. The bio section of your query letter provides your related credits and explains how you are qualified to write this particular piece. You close by asking simply, "May I have the assignment?"

Once your query is done, you can send it to editors in the traditional way, via U.S. mail with an SASE enclosed for the reply. Or, if their guidelines allow it, you may send that query pasted directly into an E-mail. The latter method might get you a quicker reply—but it's oh so easy for that quick reply to be a negative. In addition, if an editor wanted to send you guidelines, or any kind of printed material or sample copy, an E-mail wouldn't always allow for that. So take that into consideration when approaching your markets. Markets that are strictly on-line will most likely be the ones to prefer E-mail transmissions.

Marketing Your Work

Do You Need an Agent?

Here freelancers go it alone. Most agents will not handle articles, unless you are one of their famous clients who also writes books. There is a lot of work involved in selling an article. A commission of 15 percent of $150 to $2,000 or so doesn't make it worthwhile for an agent to enter this arena.

Successful freelancers are aggressive marketers. The more query letters or articles you have circulating, the better your chances of landing assignments. Send out query letters on a regular basis—full-time freelancers reveal they send out forty to fifty query letters a week. That's a lot of work, but no one said it was easy! Not all query letters, though, are for brand-new article ideas.

Resales

Successful freelancers have learned that writing an article, selling it to a publication, then writing another article to sell to the same or another publication is a slow way of going about earning a living. They count on being able to sell the same article to more than one publication.

When they come up with an article idea, they plan ahead: how many different markets can this article target?

Unless a publication has bought all rights (and you don't want to sell all the rights to your articles), you are free to resell your article as often as you can. However, the rule is that you must approach only noncompeting markets. For example, your travel piece on the "Ten Most Popular Vitamins" could appear in the health sections of both the *Washington Post* and the *San Francisco Chronicle*. These two newspapers do not share the same readership. But your piece on "Pyramid Power—Fact or Fantasy" could not appear in both *New Realities Ezine* and *ZenSpin*; chances are these two do share the same audience.

Reslant and Resell

The previous section cautions against selling the same article to competing publications. But there is a way to resell your pieces to similar markets—with just a little extra work. You've written a piece called "Macrobiotic Recipes for a Healthy Cat," for example, and have sent it off to either *Cat Fancy* or *Cats* magazine. Now it's time to sit back and take a second look at the article. It probably wouldn't take much work to reslant and come up with "Macrobiotic Recipes for a Healthy Dog" or to go even further for your horse, pet ferret, or your aquarium, even. A few new quotes from the appropriate experts, examples tailor-made for the publication, and you're on your way to selling the reslanted piece as many times as there are interested markets.

Religious publications are abundant and are also very good markets for reslanted articles. *Spiritual Life*, a magazine targeted mostly to a Catholic readership, might use an article on contemporary spirituality. So might the noncompeting *SCP Journal*, geared toward nonbelievers.

Writing Nonfiction Books

Articles tell a short tale. If you have more to say and have something to say you think will sell, then a nonfiction book would be the way to go.

Of approximately one hundred thousand books published each year, 85 percent to 90 percent are nonfiction. That means that nonfiction writers have many more markets to approach than fiction writers, and their chances of breaking in with that first book are much higher.

Selling, Then Writing, Your Nonfiction Book

Often nonfiction writers can sell a book based on a detailed proposal, before they sit down to write the book. If your proposal is well crafted, has all the important information, and convinces the editor you can deliver a professional manuscript, and on time, you might just find a contract coming back in your SASE.

Some editors, though, might be reluctant to offer a contract to a writer with no track record or no real expertise in the subject matter. In this case, you would have to decide if it's worth the risk to write the book on spec. If you've done your research, know that there's a place for your project on bookstore shelves, and are a competent writer, it might be worth forging ahead.

What isn't a good idea is to write a nonfiction book first, then start looking for possible publishers for it. Just as with articles, you have to write to the market—know that there's a niche out there within which your book can fit.

The following eight steps to getting your nonfiction book published will show you the ideal procedure to follow.

Eight Steps to Getting Published

Step One: Develop an Idea

Sounds simple enough, but you must make sure your idea is viable and tightly focused. The next two steps help you accomplish this.

Step Two: Do Your Research

How many other books are out there covering your subject matter? A simple search on the Internet or at the library (*Books in Print*) can answer that question right away. If there are dozens and dozens of books on the subject, it could mean your idea isn't new and original and it's been done to death.

Don't despair, though. If your book has an original slant, a fresh focus, a perspective that hasn't been covered, you might be able to keep that project alive yet. For example, there might be hundreds of books out there that cover traveling through Europe. But if your book is narrowed down and is, for example, a guide to bike tours on the continent, or walking trails, then perhaps there is room for your title, too. The narrower your focus on a well-published topic, the better your chances.

But not too narrow. What if there are very few or even no books on your topic in print? Does that mean you're a shoo-in? Possibly. It could also mean there is no interest in the topic and publishers don't want to take a chance. Say, for example, your bike tour book focuses on only one small city in an area that isn't attractive or accessible to tourists. The audience for this book would be too narrow—and that's why you didn't find other books on the subject.

Researching competing titles is only half of it. You also need to have a good idea who would buy your book and how this market would be reached. Are you considering a book on pet care? Then have a rough number of how many pet owners there are in the United States (and Canada, too, possibly) and how many pet shows are held each year where your book could possibly be sold.

Step Three: Target the Markets

After you've done your initial research and see there might be an audience for your book, you need to find the publishers you could approach with the project. *Literary Marketplace* (available in your library), *Writer's Market* (available in bookstores or on the Web), and *The International Directory of Little Magazines and Small Presses* (the address for purchasing this book is provided at the end of this chapter) are the best places to start.

Contact likely candidates and ask them to send you their catalogs. Then you can see exactly what they've already published and where your book may or may not fit in. Also ask for their writers' guidelines, so if you do decide to approach them, you can offer them exactly what they want. For example, the guidelines will tell you their word count requirements and if they expect authors to provide illustrations or not.

Step Four: Compose Your Query Letter

Just as with article writing, your query letter for a nonfiction book must be professionally crafted. Include a summary of the book's focus, a rationale for that book—why it should be published—and why you're the one qualified to write the book—all in one page. At the end of your query, offer to send a detailed proposal.

Step Five: Send Your Query Letter

Once you have your list of potential publishers, mail your query letter with an SASE to just a few at a time. If you do get feedback on your idea, you might discover a need to revise your query. You want to make sure you haven't blitzed all the markets and have no publishers left to query.

Step Six: Craft Your Book Proposal

While you're waiting for those SASEs to come back to your mailbox, get your proposal ready. An excellent guide to help with this is Michael Larsen's *How to Write a Book Proposal* (Writer's Digest Books). In brief, your proposal should include the following sections.

A. Proposal Table of Contents

This is to show what sections you have included in your proposal and on what page of the proposal each can be found. (It is not the table of contents for your proposed book.) You would include the following topic headings (items B through J) in the proposal table of contents.

B. Introduction/Overview

This section is where you try to hook the publisher's interest. It should explain your book and make it sound compelling enough that the publisher will want to read the rest of your proposal.

C. The Competition

Here you want to show that there's a gap in the marketplace for your book. You should list all the competing titles out there and discuss why your book is both different and better, what need your book fills that the others do not.

D. The Market

In general, it's the publisher's job to know the market—they are already well aware of school and public libraries, for example. But, if you know about special outlets for selling your proposed book, mention them here. Also, be sure to discuss the demographic and general profile of the reader of your book.

E. Format

In this section, explain how your book will be laid out—how many parts, how many chapters, whether illustrations are required. If you're proposing a cookbook, for example, give the publisher an idea of how many recipes will be in each chapter and what kind and how much additional information will be included with each recipe.

F. Author Bio

Focus your bio on the areas that show you are qualified to write this book. If your proposed book is a history of a particular region and you happen to be a Ph.D. historian, an expert in the field, then highlight that. Are you proposing a self-help manual for those living "alternative lifestyles"? Make sure you're a qualified professional who has counseled hundreds, if not thousands, of people on these issues.

What if you're not an expert in any particular field, and you just have your own experiences from which to draw? Then you've got a tough sell on your hands. Give your proposal extra credibility by pointing out that you'll be providing quotes and interviews with experts (both here and in the format section) and also consider finding an expert in the field who will coauthor the book with you or provide a foreword.

G. Sample Table of Contents

Provide in your proposal a sample table of contents, naming each chapter. You can mention a few of the chapter topics—but no need to go into great detail here. You'll do that in the next step. The sample table of contents is to provide the person considering your proposal with a quick look at what your book will cover.

H. Chapter Summary

Provide a brief, tightly written paragraph or two, summarizing the focus of each chapter. Avoid a common mistake—don't begin each chapter summary with "Chapter 1 includes . . . Chapter 2 includes . . ." Jump right into the meat of each chapter.

I. Delivery

Some proposals include a section letting the publisher know when you think you can finish and deliver the manuscript. However, this might show ignorance of the publisher's schedule. If you estimate you might need eighteen months and the publisher wants to go to press in a year, your declaration might put you out of the running.

If the book is already completed, then this section would say something to the effect that the manuscript can be delivered upon request. However, it's not a good idea to let the publisher know that the manuscript is finished. The point of the proposal is to get a contract before you actually write the book. What if you've written a two-hundred-thousand-word tome and the publisher is interested only in sixty thousand words? Certainly, you'll be willing to edit it down—but it's better to wait until you receive a response from your proposal before explaining you might have a monster on your hands. A publisher might be interested in your book and want to work with you, producing the finished product. Announcing a fait accompli might make the publisher feel pushed out of the loop. The delivery section of your proposal is optional and often best omitted.

J. Sample Chapters

Some proposals include one or two sample chapters, to give the publisher an idea of your book's focus and the style of writing. However, if you're hoping to land a contract based on the proposal, this is a lot of work to do on spec. If you've already written the book, then by all means, include samples. If not, then omit this section and wait to be asked.

Step Seven: Send Your Cover Letter

If you've sent off a one-page query letter first and received requests for the detailed proposal you offered, make sure to include a cover letter that performs the following three functions:

- Reminds the publisher that your material is solicited

- Reminds the publisher in a sentence or two what your proposed book is about

- Reminds the publisher who you are and what qualifies you to be proposing this book

Keep the cover letter to less than a page. Make sure you have all your contact information, including your E-mail address. And don't forget to include an SASE for either the return of your proposal or a response.

Step Eight: Write the Book

If all has gone well—you did your research, sent out your queries, and followed through with requests for your proposal—you might just find yourself with a contract and a due date. Now it's time to write that book. Don't be afraid of discussing the focus or approach with your editor. But, as with any writing project, you must apply bottom to chair—sit there and do it.

Do You Need an Agent for Nonfiction Books?

You've just read the Eight Steps to Getting Published, and now you're wondering why contacting agents was not mentioned. While fiction writers more often than not fare better with an agent representing them, nonfiction writers can often approach publishers alone. (Article writers have no choice—agents won't handle articles.)

There are many more publishers who handle nonfiction than their fiction counterparts, and often these publishers are open to accepting submissions directly from the writer. In fact, many of the smaller presses rarely are approached by an agent and are not used to working with them. This in part is because most agents prefer to work with the big publishing houses, where advances and subsequent print runs and sales are usually higher.

If your project is of global interest, you could approach agents first—following the same steps mentioned earlier. But if your project fits more into a niche market, don't be hesitant to go it alone.

Earnings

Articles

Most writers are thrilled to see their bylines—that is, their names in print—giving them credit for an article. And to writers, nothing is more exciting than the finished product, getting to see their stories in print. But even more important to the full-time writer is the paycheck that makes this writing life possible. In the 1700s, Samuel Johnson summed it up by saying that no one but a blockhead writes except for money.

It is a well-established fact that writers for the most part are underpaid. Salary surveys conducted by the Author's Guild, National Writers Union, and others suggest that only 15 percent of freelancers earn more than $30,000 a year.

Publications usually pay by the word—anywhere from one cent to $1 or $2. This doesn't mean you can earn more money by writing longer articles or padding your piece with extra words. In their guidelines, publications state their minimum and maximum word count requirements—and the editors are certainly professional enough to recognize padding when they see it.

Other publications pay a flat fee—$5 to $1,000 or more for an article, with the national magazines at the top of the scale. (And that's why it's much harder to break into these markets—the competition is fierce, and many of them work only with staff writers.)

Some smaller publications pay only with complimentary copies and a byline. When you query an idea and are given the assignment, discussing payment is usually the next step—and negotiating for more money at this point is not inappropriate. In fact, editors often say they are quite willing to negotiate—and are surprised more writers don't come out and ask for higher fees.

Let's face it. Writers often go into this business not fully understanding that it is a business. A writer's expertise is with the written word—not with dollar signs and decimal points. But to be a successful freelancer, you have to overcome that mind-set, develop a strong business sense, and remember you are selling a valuable product. Yes, there's a lot of competition—other writers selling equally valuable products. And editors can pick and choose who to work with. But, if you approach the subject with tact and confidence, you won't turn off an editor and send them looking elsewhere. Your article is something they have decided they want—they might have even given you input into what they'd like to see in it—and there is no reason you shouldn't be paid fairly for it.

Having said that, some of the smaller publications just don't have the budget to pay you what your piece is worth. If a byline and a credit are important to you, go ahead with the sale. But be sure to negotiate one-time rights so you can sell the piece elsewhere for additional income.

Some publications will accept photographs or other illustrations with your article—and pay you for each one. Sometimes you'll earn more for your photos than the actual article! One travel writer, who was also an accomplished photographer, realized this early on—and stopped writing articles to focus on creating a stock library of color slides to supply to magazines and newspapers.

As mentioned earlier, resales are the bread and butter for freelance writers. When investigating ideas for articles, keep resale and reslant possibilities in mind. You'll make more money in a cost-efficient manner selling one article to ten different publications than writing ten different pieces and trying to market each of them only once.

It is important to keep in mind that publishers are notoriously slow to pay for your material. Articles are usually paid for in one of two ways: upon acceptance or upon publication. "Upon acceptance" could mean the check will be cut right away—or it could mean four to six weeks before the accountant gets around to it. "Upon publication" means that your check will not be issued until the article appears in print. That could be six months to a year from the time you received your acceptance letter. Often your check will be mailed to you with the sample copy of the issue in which your material appears. With this long lag, you can see how important it is to have as many articles as you can circulating to the different publications.

Occasionally a publication might purchase your article and promise to run it—then for a variety of reasons, decide not to use it after all. Maybe an on-spec article they like better on the same topic just arrived, or they changed the focus of the publication or decided a topic was too controversial or is now passé. When this happens, some publications pay a kill fee—perhaps 15 percent to 25 percent of the agreed-upon fee for the article. This should be paid willingly and amicably—if they state in their market listings or guidelines that they offer a kill fee. But at least one editor has been quoted as saying, "Yes, we pay kill fees, but then we wouldn't work with that writer again." It's not fair, that's true, but again, there's not much you can do about it. Over time, you will learn to pick and choose the editors you submit to and continue to work with. Establishing good relationships with editors is in part how successful writers keep those assignments and checks coming in.

Books

Some contracts for nonfiction books provide an advance against royalties. Others offer a work-for-hire or flat-fee arrangement. This means that whatever you're paid up front for the book will be all you'll see. If the book goes on to be a bestseller, your bank balance will have no cause to celebrate.

Sometimes you have no choice, and if you think sales might be minimal—it's a small press with short press runs and limited distribution—a flat fee is not a bad idea.

If the publisher is confident and plans a fairly large initial press run of say ten thousand or more, and offers an advance against royalties, you can hope to see some checks down the road, once the advance is earned back and your royalty payments kick in.

Statements are usually issued twice a year, and it could be a year or so before sales have earned back the advance.

Dollar amounts are hard to pinpoint. Some of the small presses offer no advance at all, just a royalty percentage. With this scenario, you have no money coming in while you're writing the book, but at least you won't have to wait too long to earn back a nonexistent advance. In theory, you should receive your first check when the next royalty period is due, probably six months from the time your book is on the market.

Other small presses offer advances that range from $500 to $3,000 or so. A large publisher might advance a new writer as high as $10,000 to $25,000 or sometimes more, if it's a hot topic and the sales team predicts healthy sales.

Keeping Track of Your Submissions

Accurate record keeping is an important aspect of your writing business. You don't want to submit the same article or book proposal twice to the same editor. Develop a system for yourself that allows you to keep track of possible markets, submission dates, responses, publication dates, payment, and rights information.

Some writers use an index card system; others use computer software specifically designed for this purpose. The more organized you are, the more successful you'll be.

Writing in Cyberspace

As mentioned earlier, there are many Internet publications out there—magazines, newsletters, and more—that never see a piece of paper. Some pay, some don't. Some E-book publishers will actually charge writers to post material in hopes someone will want to buy it. (This is nothing short of a vanity press and should be avoided. Legitimate publishers pay writers, not the other way around.)

There are also many websites needing content. Write a regular column for an astrology site, explain New Age terms to a metaphysical site. Just fire up your favorite search engine, key in your search words, then make contacts with sites that seem appropriate. (For more information, see Maggie Anderson's first-hand account in Chapter 2. She writes for many on-line areas.)

Editing and Publishing

As with any publication, New Age publications utilize the services of a wide range of publishing professionals—from top executive to senior and associate editors to graphic artists, Web designers, and proofreaders.

Publishers usually expect their personnel to be experienced and well trained in a variety of platforms. Although a college education isn't a requirement, with all the competition out there from graduates with bachelor's degrees in English, communications, and journalism, the degree would keep you in the running.

Conduct an Internet search for publishers and jobs in publishing and see what you come up with. The Internet has become the best thing since the Yellow Pages—with such a broad range of listings, both by topic and geographic region. The world is there for you to approach!

Bookselling

A book idea starts with a writer, who nurtures it until it's a viable project, nudged across the computer screen until enough pages print out to form a manuscript.

Agents try to sell the idea to editors, and editors and other publishing company staff work together to transform the idea into print form.

But it's booksellers who get the idea out to the public. Read more about a career in New Age bookselling in Chapter 6.

Firsthand Account

Joseph Hayes, Freelance Writer

Joseph Hayes writes features for a variety of magazines and newspapers. His articles cover people, food, computers and technology, travel, music, and writing about writing. His work has appeared in the following publications: *Fiction Writers Guideline, Gila Queen's Guide to Markets, Inklings/Inkspot, iUniverse.com Nonfiction Industry Newsletter, January Magazine, Jerusalem Report, MaximumPC, Moments Aboard Spirit Airlines, MyMatcher.com, Orlando Magazine, Orlando Sentinel, Poets & Writers, savvyHEALTH, Venture Woman,* and *Writer's Journal.* His first article was published in January 1997.

Getting Started

"It began as an outgrowth of my other profession: I was a corporate sales trainer for many years, and as such, I developed a skill at taking complicated technical terms and processes and putting them down on paper so they were understandable to ordinary people. My first love will always be fiction writing, but I've been able to take those talents and use them to create what is called creative nonfiction.

"I got started by calling up the local newspaper and speaking to a regional editor. I suggested several concrete story ideas about the community I live in. She liked one, told me to write it, and I've been writing steadily ever since."

What the Work Is Like

"My first duty involves personal accountability—weighing the necessities of landing paying assignments with social responsibility gets high marks. Will I take any assignment, as long as it pays? So far the answer is no.

"Then the duties of the professional writer come in—meeting deadlines, being obligated to deliver the best work you are capable of, regardless of the subject matter, and being in contact with editors once they give you assignments so they know what you're up to.

"I love my job. Not only do I get to (and *have* to) set my own schedule, but I have the opportunity to meet incredible people, people whom I wouldn't ordinarily get to know. The hours are long, and there can sometimes be long gaps between paydays, but I'm paid for doing something I've always wanted to do.

"Mostly I write about people—about life. I like to tell stories about ordinary people who do extraordinary things: the guy who sells UFO abduction insurance, the woman who takes photographs of people's auras, the ex-police officer who teaches the bagpipes. My travel articles are about places a tourist wouldn't normally go; my technology pieces are based on helping people understand what on earth modern technology means to them. Bottom line, I'm a storyteller, whether I'm doing it in a piece of fiction or a newspaper.

"Ninety-five percent of my work is generated by ideas I send out. This is called the query process. If it's an editor I know or have worked with before, I will pick up the phone and give my idea a quick pitch. If it's a new editor or a new publication, I send a letter with a detailed but brief summary of the idea, along with copies of similar articles that I've published before—my 'clips.'

"In either case, it means that you have to have a very clear and specific idea of what story you want to do. Saying 'I'd really like to do an interview with a band' isn't an idea; it's a daydream. 'I've met the drummer for Back Street Boys, and he'll talk to me about the band' is a legitimate article pitch.

"How one decides who to approach depends on what you write. By looking at guidebooks such as the *Writer's Market* and visiting your local newsstands, you get to see which magazines print articles on topics you can write about, which magazines pay, and which ones accept pieces from freelancers.

"A freelancer's life goes through cycles: periods of waiting for work, followed by frantic episodes of meeting deadlines. A query can go unanswered for months, but when an editor finally decides he wants the work, he wants it yesterday. This year I had enough time to go on a two-week vacation, and when I got back home, there were six contracts waiting for me, all due in a month!

"I truly believe the job is what you make it. You can be as busy (and successful) as you want to be. Even at this stage, I'm still learning to pace myself when it comes to getting work, and I think I could be doing twice as much writing as I'm doing now if I wanted to but at the risk of doing less quality work than I demand from myself. As it is, I will often put in a twelve-hour day, between writing, researching, and interviewing."

Upsides and Downsides

"The best part is the freedom, working for myself. Of course, I don't work for myself, I work for magazines and newspapers and editors, but each job has a different boss, and I know if I have a bad experience with one boss, I need not work for him or her again.

"The thrill of stepping up to a magazine rack and seeing your name on the stands is one that I hope will never wear off.

"The bad side is waiting—waiting for an assignment, then waiting for a check. Keeping track of your submissions, your billing, even your expenses, can be tiring and overwhelming, but it's part of the job. A writer only writes part of the time. The rest of the time is spent with details and selling yourself.

"It can also be lonely—most of the time you are in your office, facing a screen, talking to yourself. And there are times when you have to convince your friends and family that you are actually working even though you are home, and they must respect that."

Earnings

"Someone just starting out can expect to earn very little, if any-thing. Most freelance writers do it as a part-time thing and very often get no pay at all for their work. It's part of establishing yourself in the business and getting experience.

"Once your reputation and skill warrant it, a freelance feature writer can expect to find widely varying pay rates—everything from five cents to a dollar a word is typical (and some lower than that), while the big, national magazines will pay thousands of dollars an article, but that's a tough group to join."

Advice from Joseph Hayes

"First of all, love language. Love to write. Some writers say they love having written, but hate writing. Such a waste of time! Enjoy every part of the process, of sitting in front of the computer or typewriter or notepad, and you'll never suffer from what is called writer's block.

"The article writer should be, first and foremost, an article reader—be aware of styles of writing, of how things are said. Be a reader, be voracious. Devour facts. Some people keep journals or diaries and jot down observations of people and places. Learn how to put those observations on paper; it's called finding your voice. Writer and teacher Larry Bloom says that voice, the per-sonal voice of the writer, is the most important part of any story—that is, what you yourself add to the article. Remember that only you can tell the story you are telling.

"To start out, find a discussion group at your library, local bookstore, or on-line and talk about your daily encounters. Learn to listen. Call your local newspaper or church, check the clubs you belong to, ask at local businesses and see if they have newsletters you can write for. The more words you put in print, the better your words get. And most importantly, never give up!

I've been very lucky, being as successful as I've been in such a short time. Some writers put in several years of hard work before they see real success. It can be very discouraging, but it's also very rewarding."

For More Information

American Society of Journalists and Authors
1501 Broadway
New York, NY 10036

The Dow Jones Newspaper Fund
P.O. Box 300
Princeton, NJ 08543

The Dow Jones Newspaper Fund offers summer reporting and editing internships.

Fiction Writer's Connection
P.O. Box 72300
Albuquerque, NM 87195
www.fictionwriters.com

The Gila Queen's Guide to Markets
   (monthly marketing magazine)
Box 97
Newton, NJ 07860

National Newspaper Association
1627 K Street NW, Suite 400
Washington, DC 20006

A pamphlet titled "A Career in Newspapers" can be obtained from National Newspaper Association.

National Writers Club
1450 South Havana, Suite 424
Aurora, CO 80012

For New Age publishing resources—directories, sites, magazines, teachings, articles—visit the website: www.newageinfo.com/res/newage_data.htm

CHAPTER SIX

Profit for Prophets
Careers in New Age Merchandising

W ho knew when pet rocks and the yellow and black smile buttons went on sale years ago they'd be such big successes? (Well, maybe some of our psychics in Chapter 2 knew.)

After that came pyramids, crystals, magnets, special jewelry, special water, and more. In fact, there's a whole range of New Age products that are enjoying modest to glorious sales. You can start a new fad yourself or cash in on an existing trend.

At a loss for what product to sell or what service to offer? Try firing up Yahoo! or America Online and do a search using the keywords *New Age merchandise*. Here is just a sampling of what you'll get. The list is bound to spark some ideas of your own.

- Adirondack Artworks—an artist cooperative offering Native American sterling silver jewelry (authenticity guaranteed), Iroquois Nation stone carvings, wildlife wood carvings, crystals, New Age pen-and-ink prints and originals, Indian-made beadwork, fetishes and artifacts, and gifts from Mother Earth.

- Alchemistra Ltd.—New Age spiritual products, including jewelry, healing tools, and super-ionized water.

- Atmanbooks.com Inc.—books, music, gifts, and videos about the New Age, new thought, metaphysics, alternative health, and healing and spirituality.

- The Aumara Light & Healing Circle—a place for healing and inspiration for increased health, well-being, and spiritual awareness.

- Awakening Eye, Journeys for the Soul—customized workshops for group leaders, therapists, spiritual counselors and healers who are mind, body, and spirit practitioners.

- Beyond the Rainbow: Resources for Well-being/Gifts with Spirit—free, practical information about crystals, flower essences, aromatherapy, emotional/ spiritual growth.

- Dancing Frog Jewelry—handcrafted metaphysical jewelry in sterling silver and fused glass.

- Dancing Moon Metaphysical—bookstore and gift shop for spiritual and personal growth.

- Golden Light—an intriguing strategy of mystical experiences from a woman who had two near-death experiences.

- Just Wingin' It—spiritual products from 'Angel to Zen.'

- Lytha Studios—Celtic and spiritual jewelry, clothing, and accessories, including incense and burners, hand-mixed oils, tarot cards and rune sets, candles, crystals, and ritual soaps.

- The Magical Blend—on-line catalog offering a complete selection of esoteric & metaphysical supplies, including books, tarot, oils, herbs, candles, ritual tools, symbolic jewelry, runes, and incense.

- Peaceful Paths—enlightening books, visionary artwork, spiritually nourishing music, and gifts and gift baskets in themes of spirit and wholeness.

- Planet Earth Music—fresh, evocative, magical music from all over the world.

- Psychic Choice—on-line psychic readings; classes in tarot, metaphysics, and psychic development.

- Spheres To You—more than three thousand mineral spheres used for metaphysical purposes, healing, and collecting of beautiful natural earth materials.

- Unlimited Thought Bookstore—New Age bookstore and learning center.

- Wicca Supplies Shop—quality magical jewelry, ritual tools, books, music, essential oil blends, and tools for self-transformation.

Storefronts on the Web

In addition to sparking ideas, this list of New Age product websites tells you one other thing: with the advent of the World Wide Web, there is no longer a need for a merchandiser to open a costly storefront. Dispense with all that overhead by designing a website for yourself—or hiring someone else to do it for you. You'll pay a modest monthly server fee and a few hundred dollars for a few pages. Acquire a merchant account or contact any of the cyber cash outlets (find them using an Internet search engine), submit your site to the search engines, and then you'll be up and running—in business for yourself.

Expand Your Services

As your own search will reveal, there's a lot of competition out there. So, choose your product or service carefully. Make sure you have an audience you know how to reach, if not on the Web, then through seminars or classes you offer or through some other means. Entrepreneurs think big. To make a living, you may need to offer as many related products or services as you can.

If you're a spiritual advisor with an office that clients visit, you can always display crystals or jewelry or soothing candles to sell to them. Tarot readers can try selling decks of tarot cards with fancy cases to their customers. (Don't worry. They'll still come back to you for interpretations.) Massage therapists can sell essential oils for clients to use at home. Counselors can sell books and tapes. The list is limited only by your imagination.

Storefronts with a Physical Address

Yes, it costs a lot more than a website, but opening your own store can be rewarding, both financially and spiritually.

There are three main factors you need to consider when going this route: location, location, location.

All right. You've heard that before. But it's true. You need to set yourself up in an area that is easily accessible to foot traffic, whether renting space in a mall or in a downtown shopping district.

There are two other things to consider as well—the product you'll offer and how you'll finance yourself.

First, a look at two popular enterprises—bookselling and health food stores.

Bookstores

You can have a hodgepodge of books and other products or specialize just in books. New Age bookstore sections in the chain and independent bookstores are growing like teenagers on vitamins. Enthusiasts read broadly about ancient and cutting-edge topics, keeping titles in print for many years. Closely related to the self-help field, metaphysics has spawned many how-to volumes. Print magazines also abound.

A bookstore devoted to New Age volumes could do well, depending, of course, on the area of the country you're in. Santa Fe, New Mexico? Great. Deerfield Beach, Florida? Probably not so great.

Health Food and Natural Food Stores

Natural food stores, also known as health food stores, are specialty shops that cater to a wide range of people—not just New Agers. The wider your audience, the better your business.

These stores sell a full range of healthful foods and related items such as vitamins and food supplements. Employees in natural food stores must be knowledgeable about the different foods and products and be able to answer customer questions.

Disclaimer

Once again, New Agers who are in a position to affect the emotional or physical lives of their clients have a huge responsibility. Health food stores, for one, stock a variety of products that claim all sorts of properties—from the magical to the mundane. And health food employees dispense advice as readily as trained pharmacists. But they are not trained pharmacists, and that's where the cautions come in, for the consumer and for new health food store employees.

Many health food store clerks are trained on the job. Most have not had any formal training about the products, how they work together—or how they might adversely interact with other medications.

Abigail Trafford covers this topic in her article, "Second Opinion," which appeared in the *Washington Post*, Tuesday, July 25, 2000. She says, "There is much to gain in alternative remedies. Many products hold the promise of enhancing health and mitigating symptoms of disease. And some health food stores have very knowledgeable salesclerks to guide consumers. But it's time for science to separate the wheat from the chaff in alternative remedies. Time for the FDA or some independent agency to evaluate products."

Until then, we're on our own.

The remainder of this chapter will introduce you to someone involved in bookselling and someone active in a health food store. What better way to get a feel for the business than from those already in the business.

Financing Your New Age Enterprise

Do you need to be rich to start your own business? It certainly helps. But while many enterprises require substantial backing, others, especially Internet-based concerns, could be started on a shoestring.

It's nice to have a fat bank account—or a rich uncle—but it's more important to have a good credit history. That's what lenders look at when you apply for a loan. And most of the time, starting a business requires financing. Good credit shows reliability, that you can and will pay back the loan in a timely manner. Collateral helps cement the deal.

Check in with your bank. Bank employees are familiar with a host of loan programs, especially those sponsored by the Small Business Administration. The SBA is a government-sponsored agency that helps small business, particularly those run by women or minorities. They have a lot of restrictions and qualifications—and in some instances won't fund writers or booksellers for fear of appearing to interfere with the right of free speech.

Read the firsthand account given us by former bookstore owner Joyce Kennett. She'll give you an idea of the finances involved.

Firsthand Accounts

Joyce Kennett, Bookstore Owner

From 1985 to 1990, Joyce Kennett was co-owner with her husband of the Psychic Institute, a metaphysical bookstore in Las Vegas, Nevada. Through the bookstore, they offered classes in the psychic arts and yoga.

Getting Started

"My husband and I were first employed by the store back in 1982—he as the hypnotist, and myself as a psychic. We purchased the store in 1985, but I sold it in 1990, after the death of my husband.

"I've always wanted to run a bookstore, and when this one came up for sale because of feuding partners, we snapped up the opportunity."

What the Work Was Like

"We had a double storefront loaded with books on a variety of religions, but the main focus was the metaphysical. We carried meditation music tapes and videos and stock of all sorts—incense and burners, candles, tarot cards, regular cards, joss sticks, crystals, crystal balls, runes—if you can think of a metaphysical tool, we carried it.

"We taught classes in tarot reading, psychometry, hypnosis, yoga, tai chi, and various psychic arts. We had free lectures on the psychic arts Sunday afternoons. We also had psychic affairs, offering mini-readings to the public on weekends, as well as private readings in the many psychic arts.

"We employed several psychics and two astrologers. At one point, we had three astrologers. The psychics were paid 60 percent of the reading fees, which were then $25 for a half hour, $40 for an hour. The mini-readings were $15 for fifteen minutes. Classes were usually $10 a night. The classes were taught by other psychics as well as my husband and me.

Upsides and Downsides

"My husband and I were doing what we loved, so were pretty happy, but as the business grew, we found we had to do more administration, advertising, TV and radio appearances, ordering, etc., leaving us with little time to do what we really loved—his hypnosis and my reading and teaching.

"We had to pay strict attention to stocking our shelves, maintaining jewelry, crystal, and other items, such as office supplies, bathroom tissue—everything you can think of a home needing, a business needs on a much larger scale.

"Sadly, one has to watch out for staff theft and customer theft. Antitheft mechanisms are necessary nowadays, which is a sorry state of affairs for an otherwise positive type of business."

Salaries

"As a store owner, one needs a minimum of $50,000 to start out with—to cover all the expenses. At least back in the seventies and eighties that was the amount. Now, it would be much more. Rents are very high; utilities are outlandish; property care, such as landscaping, business licenses, zoning laws and so on, adds up. The store owner is kept hopping. Any show of profit doesn't come until perhaps you are five years into the business."

Advice from Joyce Kennett

"The most important qualities a metaphysical-bookstore owner should possess are integrity and ethics. Business training is a must. Having trustworthy people to whom you can delegate some duties or authority is also a necessity.

"The best way to get started is to find a bookstore that is struggling. You might be able to get a good purchase price break, but have an accountant check their books carefully, and check out the stock very carefully as well."

Theresa Bulmer, Health Food Store Manager

Theresa Bulmer was the manager of Cabbages Health Emporium, a health food store in South Florida. It opened its doors in 1991 as a market stocking health-oriented products. They offer a line of organic produce, organic foods, and nonorganic frozen foods and groceries. They avoid food with preservatives, refined sugars, or additives. They will not sell any food that has been irradiated to prolong its shelf life.

Getting Started

"I've been into a more healthy lifestyle for many years, but I had no idea I'd end up in a health food store and really like it. I was unemployed back in 1990, and knowing very little about health food stores or the health food industry itself, I walked into a place that was being built. I got the job that same day. Ever since then, I've been led in this direction.

"I had a sales background and some skills but very little training, so I learned on the job. You'll find that a lot of people learn on the job in the health food industry. Unless you're going to school to learn about health and nutrition, you end up being self-taught.

"To me, this is a way of life. The more people who know about organic food and health, the healthier we will be as a society. The more farmers who grow organic and the more people who buy organic, the sooner prices will go down and products will be more readily available. Then more people can be turned on to this way of life.

"I know people who have gone from doctors and pills and medication and have changed their lifestyles and now no longer need the doctors and pills and medication. I'm not downgrading traditional medicine; there are many people who have been helped that way. But there are alternatives, and if we begin to look at them, and if the holistic professionals and the doctors begin to work with each other as opposed to against each other, we can change lives."

What the Work Is Like

"Cabbages Health Emporium customers are people with special diet or health needs and those who just live a natural, healthy lifestyle, including vegans and vegetarians. We have a cafe and a vegan deli, and we also cater to sports enthusiasts and body-builders, stocking several lines of sports drinks and powders and different types of vitamins and formulas. In addition, we carry a line of environmentally safe cleaning products that are biodegradable with no harsh chemicals.

"The duties of a manager vary from store to store. I do a little of everything—I order goods, take out garbage, clean bathrooms, ring up sales, work on store operating policies, and talk to brokers, sales reps, and distributors—six days a week from 7:30 in the morning to 6:00 at night. I also supervise ten employees.

"And I talk to customers and try to keep them happy. The customers are wonderful, really. They can learn from us, and we can learn from them. Someone will come in with a product I've never seen before. I'll ask what you take it for, and they'll rattle off everything the product can do, and I get really excited because I'm learning something new.

"Some of our customers are very knowledgeable, sometimes even more knowledgeable than we are, and then we have those who are clueless. They tell us it's their first time in a health food store and they don't know what they should be buying. We're all customer-service oriented here, and if anyone is unable to help a customer, we refer him or her to someone else.

"I really like this store, and I enjoy what I do. But being a store manager, even in a health food store, can lend itself to stress. You have employees underneath you, an owner above you, customers, all kinds of salespeople, and you're being pulled in a lot of different directions. You need a lot of patience, a lot of love."

Salaries

"Entry-level salaries usually are quite low, from $5 to $6 an hour, depending on your knowledge and skills and the area of the country in which you work. As you climb up the ladder, the pay scale doesn't necessarily climb with you.

"The health food business doesn't pay very well, but you don't do it for the money. You're in the health food business to be in the health food business."

Advice from Theresa Bulmer

"It's my experience that many health food stores are very open to training new employees. At Cabbages we look for certain qualities in job candidates. We want to see a good attitude, a strong interest, and willingness to learn. It's usually obvious when you interview someone, when you talk to that person.

"When trying to get a job, in addition to scanning help wanted ads, stop by the stores where you would like to work. At Cabbages we don't advertise when we have an opening. We would put a sign in the window or check around through word of mouth."

For More Information

Small Business Administration (SBA)
www.sba.gov

CHAPTER SEVEN

Sharing the Knowledge

Careers in Teaching, Consulting, and Event Planning

P roducts aren't the only way to make a profit in the New Age marketplace. Teachers instruct students in a range of disciplines, consultants help people with anything from intuitive business planning or investments to the most beneficial way to arrange office or home furniture, and event planners organize New Age and psychic fairs.

Teaching

The activities of sharing and passing on knowledge are almost as old as time itself. Everything we learned as a child came to us from our parents or caretakers. Everything they learned was passed down to them.

The active part we take in teaching and learning is exciting and stimulating. Speak to any teachers and you're sure to hear that they learn just as much from their students as as their students do from them.

Those teaching New Age subjects are providing a valuable service, enriching the lives of their students with new knowledge, personal insight, self-awareness, and growth.

Subjects run the gamut, from vegetarian cooking to astrology to refining our skills in love and relationships. Many of the topics one can teach have already been covered in previous chapters: yoga, tarot, hypnotherapy, counseling techniques, reflexology, and so on.

Training

The qualifications you'll need will, of course, depend on the subject and, to some extent, the setting. Teachers of most New Age subjects must be experts in their areas. That old cliché—"those who can, do; those who can't, teach"—doesn't apply here. A degree in education isn't required for many of the subjects and settings, but a certain skill level and an understanding of how people learn are.

For example, if you want to teach future counselors in a university setting, you'll need a Ph.D. in the subject matter as well as experience. But if you want to teach a class in Eastern cuisine or yoga, for example, and your plan is to apply to the local adult education center, being able to demonstrate your expertise and your ability to teach will impress the director more than a string of degrees.

Possible Job Settings

Teachers of New Age subjects have a wider range of possibilities when it comes to job settings than traditional teachers do. Here is just a brief list to help spark some ideas:

- Adult education centers
- Bookstores
- Churches and temples
- Community continuing education centers
- Conferences

- Home offices or classrooms

- Gyms and health clubs

- Hotels and resorts

- Medical centers

- Summer camps

- Outdoors (parks, the beach, the forest, the mountains)

- Parks and recreation departments

- Religious retreats

- YMCA/YWCA

Finding That Job

Job hunting in this field is similar to any field. You check the Internet and the classified ads in the local paper, you send out your resume and make cold calls, and you network. Often word of mouth within the community reveals job openings and provides referrals and references. Who you know will often come in handy.

But in this field, you don't have to rely on getting a job with someone else. Many New Agers are enterprising self-starters—and they create their own jobs. Here's an example.

An experienced workshop leader and speaker worked for other people for many years and developed a following. With a large mailing list of interested clients, she wrote a book and self-published it. To promote her book and earn a living, she decided to set up a series of workshops around the country. She started locally, renting meeting space in a church, making up flyers, mailing them out, and collecting the registration money for the all-day workshop. At the workshop, she provided refreshments and sold many copies of her book. The event was successful, so she moved further afield. Because her contacts in other cities were limited, though, she utilized the services of an event planner as she traveled.

Her work required a lot of travel and time away from home. But she was able to make enough money to cover her living expenses and more. Even more important, she was able to meet many people and teach her subject matter to a far wider audience than if she had stayed home. Getting the word out and earning a living were the two most important factors to this speaker, and she was successful at both.

An easier way to do something similar would be to contact New Age or metaphysical bookstores, either locally or around the country, and offer to speak. Most bookstores don't have a budget for speakers, but if you have a book or product to promote, your talks will help boost sales.

Those who can't afford to hire you to speak could hire you to teach a class or give psychic readings. (See bookstore owner Joyce Kennett's firsthand account in Chapter 6.)

As a teacher of a New Age subject, you have many options available to you, much more than the teacher of traditional subjects. Use your creativity and imagination and the answer will come to you.

Consulting

Consulting is such a broad term; we hear it used in most every field. In our minds, we probably hold an image of an older person, semiretired from some high-powered career, who now lends expertise to others who seek it. They pay the big bucks, too.

Those consultants obviously do exist, but not all fall into that stereotype. New Age consultants often help clients invest money, arrange furniture to create the best positive energy, or plan a new business. Some consultants don't use the title *consultant*. They call themselves Feng Shui experts, investment counselors, or even just astrologers, for example. For in addition to explaining personality and behavior, astrologers can also predict the best time to plan an event, change jobs, or move from one part of the country to another. (See Chapter 2.)

Earnings for Teachers and Consultants

Don't be afraid to put a decent price tag on your services. Just because the field is New Age doesn't mean your time isn't as valuable as the engineering or law consultant. In fact, you're probably a valuable commodity. Chances are the area you're in is not flooded with other people competing with you. You have specific knowledge and expertise and should be compensated for providing it. While math teachers might be a dime a dozen, how many Qigong instructors are there?

As a self-employed individual, you also have expenses you're responsible for, such as health insurance or continuing education. Make sure you figure your expenses and build them into your fee so they are covered.

If you're not sure what to charge, decide what kind of an hourly rate you need to earn to live comfortably—$35 an hour? $50? Or maybe $200? Then think about your clients. Are they affluent or struggling students or a bit of both? Can you offer a sliding scale for your services—those who can afford to pay more, will, those who can't, don't? That's the way many teachers and consultants work.

If you've read the various firsthand accounts throughout this book, you'll see the different ways New Agers deal with salary and income. It's not a subject that needs to be whispered about. Even the most selfless volunteer has to eat.

Event Planning

Not only are you a New Age enthusiast, you're an organized one. (You have to be, to be successful at event planning.)

You make to-do lists for all your activities, and you even keep track of them and check off entries as they are completed. You have the knack of being able to pull people together for an event or special occasion. If a party needs to be planned and catered, a seminar orchestrated, a luncheon meeting organized, you're the person at the helm, controlling all the various elements.

You pay attention to details, you can juggle different tasks at the same time, and as the day draws near, you not only watch everything fall into place, you make sure it does.

How can you put these valuable skills to work for you? Many such as yourself channel their abilities into organizing some of the following events:

- Psychic fairs

- New Age conferences and conventions

- Seminars

- Workshops

- Weddings

- Parties

- Associations

- Collectives

- Clubs

- Speakers' bureaus

How to Get Started

The self-employed organizer first needs to see a need or develop one. If you're a writer, you can organize seminars. If you're a plant lover, you can arrange for garden exhibitions. If you're a photographer, you can put on a community photography competition. If you're psychic, you can arrange a psychic fair.

You can also contact existing groups—writers' associations, historical associations, the chamber of commerce, bookstores, to name just a few—and let them know of your services.

Each event or organization has its own particular requirements. Here are some of the details an organizer might have to attend to:

- Raise financing

- Arrange for a venue such as a conference hall, hotel ballroom, or school gym

- Hire speakers, psychics, readers, or musicians

- Cater refreshments

- Design, write, print, and distribute promotional material

- Rent equipment or furnishings

- Keep track of registrations or guest lists

- Send confirmation letters

- Allocate seating

- Arrange for accommodations

- Arrange for transportation

Possible Job Settings

The vast majority of event planners are self-employed. Others work for hotels, the local government body or corporation holding the event, or for businesses that specialize in this particular kind of service.

Training and Becoming ISES Certified

The International Special Events Society (ISES) has chapters all over the world, most of which offer monthly educational meetings. George Washington University now offers a degree in events management. *Special Events Magazine* hosts an annual convention for three thousand event producers, with great education sessions.

Even if you don't go for a specific event planning degree, degrees in public relations, marketing, or hotel/hospitality management can prepare you to some degree. Public relations courses very often include sections on events.

To become certified, you must apply to ISES first to be eligible for certification—you will receive a form outlining the "point system" to determine whether or not you can sit for the exam. You accumulate points from years in the business, attending continuing education classes, and so on. Once you have enough points, you sit for a written exam. The whole process is not that easy, but it pays off in two ways: your respect from your peers and your standing in the event community is raised; and you can use it as a marketing tool for clients. Clients will usually be fairly impressed when you tell them what the CSEP (Certified Special Event Professional) designation means.

For more information on certification, contact the International Special Events Society at the address provided at the end of this chapter. To keep on top of what's happening in the field, you can subscribe to *Special Events Magazine*. The address is provided in the Appendix.

Firsthand Accounts

Elizabeth English, Feng Shui Consultant

Elizabeth English has been an interior designer for twenty years and has been using the techniques of Feng Shui since 1985.

She has traveled to Kyoto for observation of Feng Shui usage and techniques in Japan and has also studied the Japanese arts of haiku and ikebana.

She has consulted in clients' residences, office buildings and home offices, resorts, hotels, restaurants, and surrounding properties—yards, gardens, ponds, roads, and driveways.

She is self-employed and works out of her home office, which faces west toward the mountains in Boulder, Colorado.

A Definition of Feng Shui

"Feng Shui (pronounced fung-schway) is the ancient art of placement to direct energy flow in one's home or business. It has been used by the Chinese for more than four thousand years and is emerging in the West as a tool to create a sense of well-being in any environment.

"Feng Shui, which is based on the flow of energy called *chi*, studies the electromagnetic energy that flows in and around everything. The words *Feng Shui* literally mean 'wind and water.'

"Feng Shui practitioners believe chi mimics the flow of these elements. With knowledge of how these energy patterns work, Feng Shui experts can manipulate environments to benefit nearly every aspect of life. Using understanding of chi as the starting point, Feng Shui consultants, interior designers, and architects work to promote health, wealth, and advantageous relationships within a home or business."

Getting Started

"As an interior designer, I knew there was more to successful design than simply utilizing the standard interior design and architecture methodology, and I was searching for a more human-centered and earth-centered approach to various aspects of my projects. I picked up several books on designing with Feng Shui and knew I'd found what I was looking for. After studying the books, I looked around my own home and realized that I'd inadvertently utilized most of the Feng Shui techniques in the book, before I'd even heard the term *Feng Shui*. Apparently, I'm what's called an 'intuitive' Feng Shui practitioner.

"As an interior designer/architect, I was able to suggest the benefits of Feng Shui applications to my residential and commercial clients. I also write articles on Feng Shui for newspapers and magazines and receive job referrals from them plus, of course, word-of-mouth recommendations from former clients."

What the Work Is Like

"A Feng Shui consultant meets with the clients in their homes or businesses and spends some time getting to know them, learning what problems they're experiencing and what desires they have to improve their lives.

"A special Feng Shui compass is often used to discover problem areas and where to start fixing those areas. Usually, a set of wind chimes can be hung to bring good chi to that area, or a fishbowl, a mirror, or a fluttering red ribbon could do the trick.

"Cracked mirrors, open bathroom doors, dirty windows, doors that lead straight through the house to the back door, a huge tree in the yard obscuring the front door, a ceiling beam over a bed—all of these are chi-blocking elements and can easily be cured, by throwing away the cracked mirror, closing the bathroom door, cleaning the windows, placing a decorative screen or large plant between the front door and the back door, adding a mirror at the front door, and moving the bed.

"The pathway to the front door should be winding and inviting, there should be a pond in the backyard, there should be no mirror facing the foot of your bed, but there should be a mirror reflecting the dining table, where the family is nourished and where everyone can communicate daily. The children's beds should not be directly above the parents' bed on an upper floor, or they will not respect their parents.

"Have you ever noticed that most Chinese restaurants have large fish tanks in the restaurant, and the cash register is by the door? An uneven number of healthy goldfish in a clean tank or bowl brings wealth to the establishment, as does the cash-register at the door rather than off to the side. A screen or plants in front of the fireplace keep the good chi from going up the chimney. A pair of ducks, side by side and tied together with a red cord, bring love and faithful relationships. Making room in your closet for another's clothes could bring a new relationship. A painting of a snarling tiger at the front door will keep out people with evil intentions. A red, black, and white bowl or basket, placed in your money corner, will bring riches. These are just a very few of the many, many Feng Shui elements that consultants must know. Each case, however, is different for the individuals who live in the home or work in the business.

"I find my information through my library of books on Feng Shui. I also subscribe to magazines on Feng Shui and regularly check in to read the messages at Feng Shui on-line websites.

"I'm a freelance Feng Shui consultant, so the hours vary widely, but usually a job is one to two hours of consultation with the client, then another hour or two of visiting the home or business, then maybe four hours or less of research and design, then another two hours with the clients in the home or business going over the changes needed. Often the client will want you to make those changes happen for them, so you move furniture, change paint colors, bring in plants and mirrors and wind chimes and goldfish bowls and install them, and remove offending items or cover them.

"Most people want more money and better health and relationships, and sometimes their entire home or business is a disaster of bad chi, so you may need to spend more hours. But often the job can be done in a single day. The fees are generally about $1,000 to $2,500 a day, plus expenses. Occasionally, a client will call in a Feng Shui consultant before they move to a new home or business, and this gives you and the client the chance to set things right from the beginning or to advise them not to move into the new location at all."

Upsides and Downsides

"I love doing Feng Shui because I can help people improve their lives in a simple manner. Being a Feng Shui practitioner and consultant is a wonderful job, and it's very fulfilling and creative, especially when combined with my knowledge of interior design, architecture, and landscape design. When I finish a job, I have the opportunity to know that I've really helped the clients, and the clients can see the results almost immediately. (Clients often call to tell me how their lives have changed for the better after their homes or businesses were set right for the correct flow of good chi.)

"One thing I dislike about the profession is that many people think Feng Shui is a scam, so sometimes one member of a family is reluctant to make the changes and is argumentative or has an insulting attitude toward the ancient art of Feng Shui.

"Also, there are no regular jobs as a Feng Shui practitioner, unless you're very well known and live in an area that is open to what may be considered New Age practices for health, wealth, and well-being. Some areas of the country are open to the field, such as Los Angeles, New York, Aspen or Boulder, and Santa Fe, for example. Other areas, such as Canada, Detroit, Chicago, St. Louis, and smaller Midwest towns, for example, are closed, gen-erally, to the whole concept."

Salaries

"I earn a minimum of $100 and up to $250 per hour for consul-tation on Feng Shui. Beginners should not charge as much—maybe $25 an hour for the first several years or until they've learned how to practice the art correctly, have a good feel for it, and have succeeded with truly helping at least ten clients. A full day should be charged at $1,000 to $2,500, depending on your experience, qualifications, and abilities.

"Important note: in reference to being paid for Feng Shui consultations, one should follow the traditional ways and not directly receive cash or checks in hand. The clients should be informed in advance that they are to give you the fee in cash (if possible) in a red envelope or folded into red paper as a gift in exchange for your gift (of consultation) to them; and you should be paid daily."

Advice from Elizabeth English

"I'd highly recommend that people wishing to become Feng Shui practitioners read as many books and magazines on the subject as they can get their hands on, visit the on-line Feng Shui websites, consider taking courses in the art, and practice on their own homes and workplaces and those of their friends and families.

"The qualities one must have is a wish to help others, a desire to learn at the feet of the masters, and an ability to understand human relationships to the earth and its natural chi, and how the invisible but real flow of chi affects our lives—in advanta-geous ways and in negative ways."

Mary Tribble, Event Planner

Mary Tribble is the president and owner of Mary Tribble Creations, an event planning and production company located in Charlotte, North Carolina. In 1982, she earned her bachelor's degree in art history from Wake Forest University in Winston-Salem, North Carolina. She is one of just a few dozen people in the country to have earned the Certified Special Event Professional (CSEP) designation from the International Special Event Society (ISES). She has attended countless continuing education courses through industry conventions. And she is asked frequently to speak on event planning at regional and national conventions.

Getting Started

"I was working at an advertising agency as an account executive when one of my clients asked the agency to plan a grand opening event for their new offices. As a special project, it ended up being my responsibility. It was a huge event—a black tie gala with a laser light show—and I loved every minute of the planning. I knew I wanted to be involved in events from that time on. At first, we opened a small division at the agency for event planning, but I soon went out on my own. I was twenty-four at the time.

"I started with nothing more than a Rolodex, sitting on my bed in my apartment. No computer, nothing. I received a loan from a friendly investor for $5,000, which tided me over until the checks started coming in. That was more than a decade ago.

"After about two years in business, I rented a small office and hired my first employee, who is still with me. I now have three employees, which is a gracious plenty as far as I'm concerned.

"Now that the industry has gotten so much more sophisticated, I'm not sure I'd be able to get by the way I did back then. Clients want event planners who are educated in the industry, carry all the proper insurance—and all that takes money. I have very nice offices in downtown Charlotte, and I think that adds credibility to my company.

"Now, because I've been around so long, I get a lot of my business through word of mouth—but I still have to market my services. That's usually through phone calls and sending out my brochure to prospects.

"I don't advertise much—not even in the Yellow Pages. But I'm very active in the chamber of commerce and am a member of our convention and visitors bureau and the International Special Events Society. A lot of business comes through networking with those groups."

What the Work Is Like

"It's crazy, stress filled, but fun. Here's a page torn from my calendar from last year:

7:30 A.M.—meeting with a client about a huge event we're planning for the millennium

9:00 A.M.—back to the office, reworked a budget for a wedding client. (The mother wanted it *all*, but the father had called me into his office—without his wife—to tell me what he was willing to spend.)

10:30 A.M.—meeting with a client about another event

Noon—off to exercise, then lunch at desk

1:00 P.M.—sales calls during the first part of the afternoon

2:30 P.M.—brainstorming meeting with staff interrupted by call from a client to put together an event in a week; reconvened staff to brainstorm

4:00 P.M.—work on writing up a proposal

5:30 P.M.—visit a potential rehearsal-dinner site

6:30 P.M.—home

"My days are rarely, if ever, relaxed. A typical day has three to six meetings, plus phone calls, deadlines for proposals, budgeting, worrying about payroll, dealing with employees' problems, making sales calls, creating diagrams of event layouts, trudging around construction sites, meeting with vendors and clients, fielding phone calls from people who want to pick my brain about the event biz, and so on.

"The work atmosphere is usually what I would describe as 'frantic fun.' I try to run a flexible company with a sense of humor—practical jokes are encouraged—but I expect everyone to roll up their sleeves and get the job done.

"In the busy season, I work sixty to sixty-five hours a week. When it's less busy, about fifty. My employees work about forty-five to fifty hours, since they only work events they are assigned. (I'm usually at them all.)

"Weddings can be especially difficult to plan because there are so many personalities involved. With a corporate client, I'm usually answering to just one person, and that person has usually reached a consensus with his or her staff as to what the event should be. With a wedding, the bride, the MOB (Mother of the Bride), the FOB (Father of the Bride), the in-laws, and the groom all have different expectations.

"In addition to weddings, I plan just about any kind of corporate event—grand openings, client celebrations, incentive events, employee receptions, and so on. This could be anything from an outdoor laser light show for twenty-five thousand people to an elegant cocktail party to a stage-show production. We come up with the ideas, then plan the whole thing from start to finish—invitations, catering, decorating, special effects, entertainment, and so forth. We contract all of that out, though. We don't keep lasers in stock!

"Paying attention to the details is the most important part of event planning. We can come up with all the wonderful themes in the world, but if we don't interpret them with details, they mean nothing. When we plan an event, everything—invitations, decorations, entertainment, place cards, gifts, signage—is selected to enhance the concept of the event.

"Also, the day-to-day planning is very detail oriented. We have to imagine an event from the time someone gets the invitation to how they will get there, where they will park, who will greet them, how the event will begin, and how it will end.

"For every event, we create a schedule for setup, which is a hour-by-hour outline of everything that will happen leading up to the event. Sometimes, if it's a complicated event, that document can be ten to twelve pages long.

"We also create a show schedule that outlines the event itself. Say, for instance, we are producing an awards ceremony. We'll develop a show schedule (a minute-by-minute one) that tells what person goes to the stage at what time, what they'll do or say on stage, how the lights in the house will be set, how the lights on the stage might change, what the audience is seeing on the video screen, and so on. Show schedules have to be incredibly detailed so that there's no down time on stage."

Upsides and Downsides

"What I like most about my work is the satisfaction that I've surpassed the client's dreams and expectations. The gasp factor. Also, I like the diversity—no day is ever the same—and I do get to spend a good deal of my time with creative people, brainstorming new ideas and coming up with new challenges. I also feel a rush from the stress the events create. I like to solve problems on my toes and come up with quick and innovative solutions.

"The long hours are a downside, though. It's not too uncommon for us to work eighteen to twenty hours with no break—and I'm getting too old for that! I work a lot of weekends and evenings. Other downsides are dealing with all the details of the event—which is why I have employees. I like to conceptualize the event, but the drudgery of all the phone calls and meetings on minute things can be tiresome."

Advice from Mary Tribble

"Education, education, education! Just because you planned your sorority rush parties and dances doesn't mean you can plan events professionally. We take on a great deal of responsibility when we put a thousand people in a hotel ballroom.

"Is the event safe? Does our layout meet fire codes? Are our linens, draping, candles approved by the fire department? Is the event handicapped accessible? Does the caterer meet health-code requirements? Do we have enough liability insurance?

"We have to think about workers' compensation and whether you have permission to record and/or play licensed music. Are we following union regulations? Will the electricity carry the load of the equipment we've brought in?

"Planning events is not all fun and games, and you must make sure you're providing your client with a safe and secure event. You need to stay atop of the cutting-edge trends and make sure your clients are getting the best services possible.

"In addition to education, you need hands-on experience. Volunteer on a committee for a local nonprofit organization's fund-raiser. Intern at an event-production company, hotel, or catering firm. The experience will be a great investment.

"The perfect event-planner personality? You need to be a left brain/right brain person—you need the creative side to come up with new and exciting ideas, but you also need the detail-oriented side to execute them. That's a tough combination.

"You also need to thrive on stress—and learn not to panic in bad situations. You need to be quick on your toes, and you need to be a negotiator, and you need to have a calming influence on people. Our clients need someone calm and relaxed in the face of the controlled chaos."

For More Information

Professional Associations

The Feng Shui Society
377 Edgware Road
London W2 1BT
Great Britain
www.fengshuisociety.org.uk

International Feng Shui Research Centre (IFSRC)
1340 Marshall Street
Boulder, CO 80302
www.fengshui2000.com

International Special Event Society (ISES)
9202 North Meridean Street, Suite 200
Indianapolis, IN 46260

Websites

Chinese Feng Shui
www.chineseculture.about.com/culture/chineseculture/msub53.htm

Feng Shui for Harmony and Relaxation
www.rainbowcrystal.com/atext/fs.html

SpiritWeb: "Feng Shui Giving Us Direction"
www2.eu.spiritweb.org/spirit/feng-shui-liu-01.html

Geomancy/Feng Shui Educational Organization
www.geofengshui.com

CHAPTER EIGHT

Third-Eye Private Eyes

*Careers in Paranormal
Investigation*

D o you believe in ghosts and spirits and haunted houses?
What about ESP and psychokinesis? UFOs? The Loch
Ness Monster? Big Foot?

Did you see *Ghostbusters* or *Close Encounters of the Third
Kind?* Do you watch the "X-Files"? Do books by Isaac Asimov
and Arthur Clarke excite and intrigue you?

Or maybe not. When it comes to the realm of the paranormal,
there are usually three sides on which people align themselves.
There are the believers, those who cannot be shaken from their
stands. Then there are the nonbelievers, those who would never
be convinced. Finally, there are those in between, the "Show
Me" group. They keep an open mind but would need hard evidence to move them off the fence.

The strong beliefs of some, either for or against, have led to
some interesting careers. But be forewarned—job opportunities
in this area are few and far between. Only a small fraction of
dedicated believers or debunkers have been able to carve a niche
for themselves in this controversial territory.

What Does It All Mean?

Every discipline has its own jargon. Before we forge ahead, it's a
good idea to have two few definitions in our arsenal.

Paranormal—an adjective used to describe activity outside or beyond the realm of "normal."

Parapsychology—the study of psychic phenomena.

A Little History

Interest in psychic phenomena can be traced back to early times. The first modern organizations to investigate such phenomena were the British Society for Psychical Research, founded in 1881, and the American Society for Psychical Research, founded in 1885.

Many of the early investigations conducted by these two groups tended to be unscientific and mostly anecdotal in nature. J. B. Rhine, a psychologist at Duke University in Durham, North Carolina, wanted to change the approach and methods used. He began his work investigating parapsychology in 1927. In the course of his work, Rhine coined the term *extrasensory perception*.

Duke eventually allowed him to split from the psychology department and form the first parapsychological laboratory in the country. That was in 1935. A little more than fifteen years ago, the parapsychology department and Duke University parted ways. But those carrying on Rhine's work did not want to let it die. They soon formed the Institute for Parapsychology, which is also located in Durham, North Carolina. (The address is listed at the end of this chapter.)

The Controversy

The majority of scientists outside the field of parapsychology do not accept the existence of psychic phenomena. As a result, they do not accept the discipline of parapsychology. In order to study something, there has to be something there to study.

The most weighty criticism launched against parapsychologists is that of fraud. Rhine himself discovered that one of his researchers had been faking results. The man was dismissed.

Parapsychologists counter this charge by saying that they do well in policing their own ranks.

Another charge is that parapsychologists are not trained enough to tell if a subject is committing fraud. Even amateur magicians have been known to fool investigators. Parapsychologists insist that this type of fraud happens only in an insignificant number of cases.

Other charges include shoddy experimental design, incorrect statistical interpretations, and misread data.

A study in 1988 conducted by the National Research Council maintained that no scientific research in the past 130 years had proven the existence of parapsychological phenomena. The council, however, did find anomalies in some experiments that they could not readily explain.

Parapsychologists claim that the study was biased because the members of the research committee were nonbelievers.

Another major criticism is that for extrasensory perception, psychokinesis, and other phenomena to be true, basic physical laws would have to be broken.

To counter that, some parapsychologists believe that breakthroughs in particle physics may one day provide explanations for such phenomena. Others feel that paranormal activity operates outside the realm of science.

Toward the end of his life, Carl Jung also suggested that the deepest layers of the unconscious function independently of the laws of space, time, and causality, allowing for paranormal phenomena.

Firsthand Account

Joe Nickell, Paranormal Investigator

Joe Nickell is one of the very few paid paranormal investigators in the country. He's a staff member of the Committee for Scientific Investigation of Claims of the Paranormal (CSICOP), which is based at the Center for Inquiry, a nonprofit organization in Amherst, New York.

He's had an interesting and colorful career, having worked as a private investigator, a professional stage magician at the Houdini Hall of Fame (as Janus the Magician and Mendell the Mentalist), a blackjack dealer, a riverboat manager, a newspaper stringer, a historical and literary investigator, and a writer of articles and books (see a listing in the Appendix). He has also managed to find time to earn bachelor's, master's and Ph.D. degrees, all in English literature, all from the University of Kentucky in Lexington.

He has appeared on the popular TV program "Unsolved Mysteries," debunking claims of the paranormal, and is a regular consultant for the show. He has also appeared on "Larry King Live," "Sally Jessy Raphael," "Maury," "Jerry Springer," and "Charles Grodin."

Getting Started

"I grew up with magic in the household; my father was an amateur magician. I am largely self-taught, but a retired magician helped me some.

"During my career at Houdini, before I went on to be an investigator, I met James Randi—the Amazing Randi—and he was conducting a lot of paranormal investigations. I thought what he did, exposing psychics, was interesting and exciting. I started my investigative career with surveillance, background checks, and some dicey undercover work. I was even a bodyguard for a politician. But primarily, I was a part of the cadre of young investigators for a well-known detective agency, doing the more dangerous undercover work.

"We would work in a company's warehouse—as a stock clerk, shipper/receiver, mail clerk, forklift driver—wherever they could slip us in. Our job was really to become aware of and infiltrate theft rings operating there. We'd set them up and bust them. The work was done privately and secretly. We'd assure the owners that we could get rid of the problem without the whole story coming out.

"If the story did come out, it would result in bad morale. The employees would not be happy that the bosses had sent spies in. The police would not be involved. The company would handle it themselves, fire the employees, and hope to keep the thieves out.

"Plus, the detective agency would not want its investigators to have to go to court. Once you did, and you were identified, it would mean the end of your undercover career. The agency would want to be able to use us again and again, not just one time.

"I also did surveillance work, staking out a place where we had undercover investigators. Or at times we'd be on the phone, just checking up on the background and character of different people.

"Unlike some of the guys who hated doing any of the office work, I would look for the general work whenever I was between undercover assignments.

"When you were on an undercover assignment, you were given your paycheck with the other factory or warehouse workers. Then your agency would make up the difference in your pay. You'd also receive additional danger pay on top of that.

"I also worked on insurance fraud cases. I was assigned to conduct surveillance on someone who was claiming he had a back injury. We staked out his house and watched him work on his car, photographing every move. He was bending over, darting up the steps two at a time. We documented it all."

Paranormal Investigations

"Pretty soon thereafter, I think in 1972, I had the opportunity to investigate a haunted house called Mackenzie House, a historic building in Toronto. There were various phenomena happening late at night there. The caretakers would hear footsteps going up and down the stairs—when no one was there. There were other sounds, too, Mackenzie's printing press, for example.

"I found that the sounds were all illusions. They were real sounds, but they were coming from the building next door. The buildings were only forty inches apart, and the other building had a staircase made of iron that ran parallel to the Mackenzie house stairway. Whenever anybody went up and down the stairs next door, it sounded as if it were coming from within Mackenzie House. The interesting thing to me was that no one had figured this out for ten years.

"I was writing a lot at the time and still am, but at the beginning, I discovered that the paranormal was a theme that I kept turning to again and again. There were so many intriguing questions.

"In the early seventies there were all kinds of claims—of psychics, of the ancient astronaut, theories about the Bermuda Triangle. It's a bit passé now, but at the time, I thought of them as burning questions.

"I've always been skeptical, not meaning debunking, just meaning 'prove it to me.' I began to investigate paranormal claims. I was in the Yukon Territory working as a blackjack dealer and would occasionally write a newspaper piece. One day, these guys were all claiming that they could use their dowsing rods to find gold. So I said, 'Talk is cheap. Would you do it under control test conditions?' They agreed.

"I put gold nuggets in some boxes padded with cotton; other boxes had nothing in them, some had fool's gold, some had nuts and bolts. I scrambled them all up, and even I didn't know when I picked a box out of the sack what was in it. The only way they would have known was if there had been any psychic power at work—and, of course, they failed the test miserably. I ended up writing an article about the experiment.

"I investigated situations all through college. Whenever I heard about something interesting, I'd pursue it myself. The next biggest investigation, where I made a name for myself, was with the Shroud of Turin. On my own, I decided that the image on the shroud—which was supposed to be impossible to duplicate because it's a negative image and no forger in the Middle Ages could duplicate it—could indeed be duplicated. I showed an easy way to duplicate it using a simple process, and I published my findings in several magazines, including one in *Popular Photography* magazine, which put me on every newsstand in America.

"From there and other publications, I attracted the notice of the Committee for Scientific Investigation of Claims of the Paranormal, which was founded in 1976. The committee's founder was Paul Hurtz, who worked closely with James Randi, Isaac Asimov, and Carl Sagan.

"There was a feeling that paranormal activity was being hyped on TV and in the tabloids and there was no voice to speak counter to it. CSICOP was set up to investigate—not to dismiss out of hand, not to start out to debunk, but simply to investigate claims of the paranormal. And if that meant debunking, so be it.

"I volunteered for years for CSICOP, then in 1995 I was hired full-time. The center needed a detective, a magician, a writer, and a researcher, and by hiring me, they found all of them in one.

"I'm sort of a magic detective. Parapsychologists really believe that there is some power of the mind to read people's thoughts or divine the future. In spite of what you might have read, though, there is no scientific evidence for any of this. There have been plenty of claims, but when the claims have been scrutinized, they've been found not to pan out—poor research methodology or tricksters using sleight of hand. And that's where I come in.

"But the phrase 'try to debunk' is very loaded. We go out to investigate. Invariably, we also do end up debunking.

"I was asked to be a consultant on 'Unsolved Mysteries,' for example. Most viewers think of the program as a documentary, but, in fact, it's just entertainment. They don't care whether they tell the truth or not. That's often the case. I've worked with them many times, and often they've left out important details, making it look much more serious, and if you question them on it they say, 'Well, after all, the name of our program is "Unsolved Mysteries."'

"One question 'Unsolved Mysteries' asked me to explain involved some miracle photographs that were taken at a Virgin Mary site in Kentucky. They sent me copies of the photographs, and I was able to duplicate all the effects and explain them. The pictures were made by some girls, Polaroids that showed unusual things, they thought. The girls had attempted to take a picture of the sun—when the picture came out, they had a picture of a doorway with an arched top and straight sides, flooded with light. The doorway to heaven. In fact, that shape was the shape of the camera's lens opening—a light-flooded silhouette of that aperture. At the bottom of a few of the pictures were what they thought were angel wings. In fact, those were due to light leaking into the cartridge.

"The most puzzling was a picture that had a faint image superimposed over the picture of the girls. It was some sort of chart. I kept saying it didn't sound miraculous, it sounded very human. I tried to figure out how it could get on there. CSICOP gave me $50 to buy film. No sooner had I put in a film pack, than it ejected a protector card. On the other side of the card when I turned it over, there was the chart. I had to laugh.

"Another case was a haunted Japanese restaurant in Atlanta. First, Dr. William Roll, a parapsychologist based there, was on 'Unsolved Mysteries' to investigate the phenomenon. One of the things he did was to take in a magnetometer. You ask yourself why is Dr. Roll taking a magnetometer in? Is there a body of scientific evidence that ghosts are influenced by magnetometers? No, there is not. There is not such a reputable body of scientific knowledge. But often self-styled ghost hunters take in fancy-sounding equipment, and if they get any type of glitches or movement, they assume it must be the ghost doing it.

"They can make fools of themselves. The manager of that very same restaurant told me that he knew that the magnetometer was simply responding to the iron metal in the pipes in the walls. The result of our investigation was that the ghost was mostly a lot of hysteria and hype and some of the employees playing pranks on one another.

"We're often accused of being debunkers as if we start out to do that. But here's the proof that we don't dismiss out of hand. If we did, we would not go to the Georgia restaurant to do an investigation. We'd say that it was just too silly to bother with. In fact, we do the investigations, but we get different results. Why? Because we don't take in silly equipment. We interview people, we look for evidence, we look for causes. One girl privately confessed that the reason the lights went on and off, which is something the bartender told us about, was that, when he wasn't looking, she would reach around and flip the switch. She had great fun doing that for some time.

"CSICOP doesn't just parachute me in whenever there's a rumor of something. We're nonprofit, and most of our money is donated, so we have to be very careful with how we spend it. Some of our funding comes from subscriptions to our journal, the *Skeptical Inquirer.*

"When I do an investigation for a TV show, the show usually pays for us to fly down there. I've been a guest on a lot of different shows, so often I'm the token skeptic. They put on the believers, the UFO abductees and so forth, and I get a minute at the end to say, 'Bah humbug.'

"But once I tested a psychic on the 'Jerry Springer Show.' It was a lot of fun. There were three psychics on, giving all sorts of readings, telling people about themselves. There's a trick to this; it's called cold reading. What you do is fish for info. You start off vague, then if the person gives you a little feedback, maybe he looks surprised or he nods in agreement, you pursue that. If he shakes his head or says, 'No, I don't have a brother,' then you pursue that. You actually can narrow your choices, and by the time you're through, you've convinced them that you know all about them. And if you've missed a few, you don't back off them. You say, 'Well, I think you will meet someone named Robert, and it's going to happen soon.'

"I was brought on as the skeptic to see if these people were really psychic. I said 'I have three envelopes, containing a simple three-letter word. And I also have a check for $1,000. The check is yours if you can guess or divine all three of the three-letter words.' Two of the psychics refused to cooperate. The third, who called himself Mr. B of ESP, the World's Greatest Psychic, agreed to be tested. Well, he failed the test. I had to tear up the check. There was a mixture of booing and applause from the audience.

"I am most interested in the investigative aspect of my work. I like solving the mysteries. That's the most rewarding part. I've never really been stumped. That doesn't mean that I know the answer to every mystery in the world. I've looked back through history, and sometimes I've been able to find the solution to a long ago puzzle.

"For example, there's the story about the disappearance of Oliver Lerch. As the story went, in South Bend, Indiana, in the 1890s, young Oliver was sent out to the well to get some water on Christmas Eve while everyone was gathered around the hearth and playing the piano. No sooner did he leave on his errand than the family heard him crying for help. Some thought he might even have said, 'They've got me.'

"They picked up the lantern and ran outside, following Oliver's tracks through the snow. Halfway to the well, the tracks ended abruptly. No sign of Oliver. A great mystery. How do you explain it?

"The story has been published in slews of different books and magazines on unsolved mysteries. Well, after further investigation, I found there was no such family as the Lerches. I did a deed search and found that no family named Lerch had ever owned any property in that area. Some of the stories claimed that the incident was still in the police files. Well, the police say they've never heard of it. No such story. Oliver Lerch never disappeared; Oliver Lerch never even existed. In fact, the story is more or less a plagiarized version of an old Ambrose Bierce horror story called 'Charles Ashmore's Trail.'"

Advice from Joe Nickell

"I think you should read as much of the literature as possible, particularly the skeptical literature. You're going to be misled by a lot of the believers. They'll tell you stories that simply aren't true. Their books are full of the fake Oliver Lerch stories. And they don't expose them, we do. Our journal, the *Skeptical Inquirer*, frequently reviews books and lists articles. That would be a good starting point.

"Then, it would be useful to learn something about magic. Not that everyone has to be a magician, but some of us are. It's useful in understanding how people can be fooled and what the different tricks are.

"In addition to magic, journalism, psychology, and astronomy, depending upon the area you're most interested in, would be useful. One of our people is with NASA, another with *Aviation Science* magazine. Psychology would be very good for investigating people who feel they're possessed or haunted or have been abducted by aliens. There are many different fields. We all count on each other and share. An investigation often doesn't just rely on one person. I often bring in many other experts and collaborate with them.

"As far as making a career of this, I think the best route to go would be investigating phenomena, then turning your material into articles. But I do have to caution: if you are really interested in being a freelance writer and making a buck, you need to be on the other side of the belief coin. You can sell a ghost story far easier than you can sell one that debunks it. (For more information on writing careers see Chapter 5.)

"But if truth and honesty matter to you, you will not sell out. You will report fairly and thoroughly."

Training

There are very few university programs in this country now devoted to training parapsychologists or their counterpart debunkers. The sixties and seventies saw a surge of popularity in these areas, but most have now gone by the wayside. Readers will have to utilize their finely tuned sleuthing skills to track down existing programs. Three leads have been given to you at the end of this chapter: the Institute for Parapsychology, American Society for Psychical Research (both mostly for believers), and the Center for Inquiry (mostly for nonbelievers).

Joe Nickell offers seminars and workshops under the auspices of the Center for Inquiry. The programs cover investigative techniques, magic used by mind readers and mentalists, and how to detect them, as well as classes on miracles and other interesting phenomena.

For More Information

Professional Associations

American Psychological Association
750 First Street NE
Washington, DC 20002

American Society for Psychical Research
5 West Seventy-third Street
New York, NY 10023

Center for Inquiry
P.O. Box 703
Amherst, NY 14226

Institute of Parapsychology
402 North Buchanan Boulevard
Durham, NC 27701

International Security and Detective Alliance
P.O. Box 6303
Corpus Christi, TX 78466

Further Reading

Writing and Editing

The Chicago Manual of Style (University of Chicago Press)

Your Novel Proposal: From Creation to Contract, by Blythe Camenson and Marshall J. Cook (Writer's Digest Books)

Guide to Literary Agents (Writer's Digest Books)

Insider's Guide to Book Editors, Publishers, and Literary Agents, by Jeff Herman (Prima Publishing)

The International Directory of Little Magazines and Small Presses (Dustbooks)

Magazine Publishing Career Directory (Gale Research, Inc.)

Market Guide for Young Writers (Writer's Digest Books)

Novel and Short Story Writer's Market (Writer's Digest Books)

Poet's Market (Writer's Digest Books)

Writer's Digest Magazine (Writer's Digest Books)

Writer's Market (Writer's Digest Books)

How to Write a Book Proposal, by Michael Larsen (Writer's Digest Books)

How to Write Irresistible Query Letters, by Lisa Collier Cool (Writer's Digest Books)

Massage

Mosby's Fundamentals of Therapeutic Massage, by Sandy and Sandra Fritz (Mosby Year Book)

The Complete Body Massage: A Hands-On Manual, by Fiona Harrold, photographs by Sue Atkinson (Sterling Publishing)

Loving Hands: The Traditional Art of Baby Massage, by
Frederick Leboyer (Newmarket Press)
The Art of Touch: A Massage Manual for Young People, by
Chia Martin, photographs by Sheila Mitchell (Hohm Press)
*The New Guide to Massage: A Guide to Massage Techniques
for Health, Relaxation and Vitality,* by Carole McGilvery
and Jimi Reed (Lorenz Books)
*The Complete Illustrated Guide to Massage: A Step-By-Step
Approach to the Healing Art of Touch,* by Stewart Mitchell
(Element Books, Ltd.)

Natural Medicine

The Encyclopedia of Natural Medicine, by Michael Murray,
N.D., and Joseph Pizzorno, N.D. (Prima Publications)
*Directory of Herbal Training Programs and Recommended
Reading List* (American Herbalist Guild)

Feng Shui

*The Complete Illustrated Guide to Feng Shui: How to Apply
the Secrets of Chinese Wisdom for Health, Wealth, and
Happiness,* by Lillian Too (Element Books, Inc.)
Interior Design with Feng Shui, by Sarah Rossbach (Viking
Penguin)
Feng Shui for the Home, by Evelyn Lip (Heian International
Publishing, Inc.
*Feng Shui Handbook: How to Create a Healthier Living &
Working Environment,* by Master Lam Kam Chuen (Henry
Holt & Company)
Practical Feng Shui for Business, by Simon Brown (Ward
Lock)

Special Events

Special Events Magazine
Miramar Communications
23815 Stuart Ranch Road
Malibu, CA 90265

Paranormal Investigation

Extrasensory Deception, by Henry Gordon (Prometheus
    Books)
Pseudoscience and the Paranormal, by Terence Hines
The Skeptical Inquirer (Center for Inquiry, Amherst, New
    York)
Secrets of the Supernatural, by Joe Nickell (Prometheus
    Books)
Looking for a Miracle, by Joe Nickell (Prometheus Books)
Camera Clues, by Joe Nickell (University of Kentucky Press)
Detecting Forgery, by Joe Nickell, (University of Kentucky
    Press)

About the Author

B lythe Camenson is a full-time writer with more than four dozen books to her credit, most on the subject of various careers. Camenson is also the coauthor of *Your Novel Proposal: From Creation to Contract* (Writer's Digest Books) and director of Fiction Writer's Connection, a membership organization for new writers (www.fictionwriters.com). She currently lives in Albuquerque, New Mexico—the Land of Enchantment.